Treasures Against Time

Paramahansa Yogananda
with Doctor and Mrs. Lewis

Brenda Lewis Rosser

Borrego Publications
Borrego Springs, California

Copyright ©1991 by Brenda Lewis Rosser

All Rights Reserved. No part of this work may be reproduced or transmitted in any form by any means, electronic or mechanical, including photocopying and recording, or by any information storage or retrieval system, except as permitted in writing from the publisher.

Borrego Publications, P.O. Box 31, Borrego Springs, California 92004

Library of Congress Catalog Card Number: 91-71815
0-9629016-0-1

Printed in the United States of America
First Edition

Dedicated to Mildred Margaret Lewis
for her strength, love, and wisdom

Table of Contents

Preface by Brenda Lewis Rosser   vii
Foreword by John Rosser   xi

1. **Mildred Lewis Reminisces**   1
   Mildred Lewis Meets Swami Yogananda, 1 • Sister Yogamata Meets Swami Yogananda, 2 • Doctor Meets Swami Yogananda, 3 • God's Light and the Rolling Pin, 4 • Mildred Lewis Becomes a Disciple, 5 • The Three Tea Leaves, 6 • The Drive Around Mystic Lake Parkway, 7 • The Boarding House: Winter, 1921, 7 • Organs, Limeade, and Tasty Indian Food, 8 • The Stanley Steamer Story, 10 • The First Flower Ceremony, 12 • Mohawk Trail, 13 • The First Ashram: Waltham, 14 • No Secrets, 15 • The First Advertisement, 15 • "Sit Down, Swamiji," 16 • The Years Speed By, 17 • The Icy Road, 19 • The Depression Years, 20 • The Guru's Blessing, 21 • God's Instant Help, 21 • Prayer on Stair Landing, 22 • Enveloped in a Blue Light, 23 • The Guru's Intercession, 24 • The Move to California, 25 • The Arizona Flagstone Sidewalk, 26 • Working in the Greenhouse, 27 • Doctor's Hat, 28 • Watermelon Story, 30 • Remembering Sister Gyanamata, 31 • Doctor's Unceasing Dedication, 32 • The Borrego Retreat, 32 • The Smallest Desire, 34 • The Borrego Retreat Evolves, 35

2. **Doctor Lewis Reminisces**   41
   A Five-Hour Meditation at Plum Island, 45 • Master Takes Care of Doctor's Family, 47 • A Time of Great Blessings, 48 • The Master Helps Doctor and His Family, 48 • Doctor Nearly Gets Wet, 49 • The Master Rescues Doctor's Health, 52

3. **Letters from Paramahansa Yogananda**   55

Paramahansa Yogananda wrote many letters over the years (1921–1951) to Doctor and Mildred Lewis. Offering a rare and intimate account of the Guru with two of his earliest disciples, ninety-seven letters are presented.

The Spirit behind the Words
The next three chapters are informal talks given by Doctor Lewis. Paramahansa Yogananda told a group attending one of the SRF services, "I am glad you attend Doctor's lectures. He gives not only the words, but the Spirit behind the words."

4. **Divine Friendship**   193
God's Love is Unconditional, 195 • Recalling the Master's Letter, 196 • Family Love Becomes Transmuted into Divine Love, 198 • Master's Rules for Friendship, 199 • Guru-Disciple Relationship, 200

5. **Intellect versus Intuition**   203
Stilling the Mind, 206 • Comparing the Two Approaches, 208 • Developing Intuition, 210

6. **The Cosmic Dream**   213
Breaking the Cosmic Dream, 215 • The Materialized Thought of God, 216 • Meditation is the Key, 219 • Attachment Brings Sorrow, 220 • The Role of Intuition, 224

Photographs from the Family Album   227
Letter from Swami Sri Yukteswar   228

7. **Addenda**   229
Doctor's Sister Dolly Reminisces   230
Letter from Ananda Mohan Lahiri   233
Two Letters from Banamali Lahiri   237
Music by Doctor Lewis   241

Preface

I can think of no more a difficult assignment than to write about one's mother and father in an objective way. How can one be objective when one has had a great affection, respect, and indeed reverence for their parents? From my years of association with great spiritual people, I have come to the conclusion that they are the most misunderstood of all souls who trod this earth. And yet they possess the character-qualities most people try to emulate: they are calm, calmer than most; they are kind, kinder than most; they are understanding, more understanding than most; and they possess wisdom far beyond the attainment of those who do not live the spiritual life and perhaps know nothing about it. And so when my mother, Mildred Lewis, enjoined me to put together a work that would reflect the early days of Paramahansa Yogananda and the relationship of his two earliest disciples, it was indeed a titanic task I faced.

As many loving children do, I always kept away from the thought that my mother would one day leave this earth. And so when we worked together (from 1966 on) to assemble the notes and letters pertinent to the manuscript we were planning, I always felt that she would be with me to guide me through the difficult parts and to remember those things that I had forgotten—she had a prodigious memory.

My mother felt that printing this work, apart from Self-Realization Fellowship, was what should be done, for there was no reason for "extra hands" working on it, when we had all the facts and figures in our possession; besides, first-hand accounts can not be gainsaid.

Possessed of keen discrimination, my mother selected those letters from Paramahansa Yogananda which would be of spiritual importance and inspiration. To this she added stories from her experience with the Guru which would be of interest to the general readership. A novelist once wrote that everyone is looking at the world through his own emotional prism, and so when spiritually advanced individuals speak first-hand about their experiences with a Guru or a great disciple, it carries a message that could not possibly be transmitted by a young editor.

I never detected in her any ego or desire to magnify the Lewis name. Conversely, her great pleasure was to live in Borrego as much as she could, as a needed break from a busy schedule, which included many interviews and activities during her years at Encinitas and, later on, at her home on the grounds of the San Diego Temple. Therefore, this book does not represent any group or organization that would disseminate the teachings of Paramahansa Yogananda in any way.

You will find that the letters to my mother and father from Paramahansa Yogananda, as well as the stories, speak for themselves. Many of the letters are completely unedited. Perhaps some of our readers have not heretofore seen the letters of the Guru in unedited form, although there are several in the work, *Mejda,* by Sananda Lal Ghosh, printed by Self-Realization Fellowship. Our purpose in publishing them in this form is to provide the truthseeker with a realistic picture, glimpsing both the radiant Divinity of the Guru and the warm humanity he manifested in all his actions. It is hoped that these letters will reveal something of the Divine relationship which bonded the Guru and two of his earliest disciples.

In earlier times, some events and stories revealed in the

book would not have been published. Those privileged to be present when the words were uttered would simply have kept them as silent treasures in their hearts. (It is evident that some of the teachings of a true Guru can not be transmitted by the written word, but only by the spoken word of the Guru to disciple; however, one should not be discouraged by this fact and the fact that the Guru is not with us in the physical form. If one follows the true teachings of the Master, one will find more blessings than he/she can sometimes hold.) Some of the aforementioned utterances are written to provide further insight into the guru-disciple relationship and to prevent certain distortions which might occur in the mass dissemination of sacred teachings.

It is difficult for me to categorize my father as a saint, for he was my dearest friend, protector, and guide. But as the years have passed, and I have reflected on his spiritual experiences and the fact that he never spoke of things he had not realized, I have come to the conclusion that he was a saint of the highest order.

Lahiri Mahasaya and Swami Sri Yukteswarji were householders, carrying the blazing spiritual torch of Self-Realization down through the years. My father, as a householder, picked up that torch and carried it high during his entire life, lighting the world with the hope that those burdened with heavy worldly responsibilities can still find God.

If the reader will kindly excuse the reference to myself, I would like to state that my life has been of service. I never entertained the thought that I would one day be asked to write a book. All I know is that it is God's will that it be written, and those who are touched by Him, and only those, will see the full import of these writings.

Those who know me know well that I could not have completed this manuscript without assistance. I gratefully acknowledge the support of Mr. Ed Martin, whose talent in graphics arts and publishing brought together those aspects of the book; however, the guiding hand and supreme effort of Mr. James M. Roberts, deserves the highest praise, for it was only through his friendship and diligence, plus his inquiring nature into the spiritual life, that the manuscript was finally sent to press.

Brenda Lewis Rosser
March 26, 1991

Foreword

Since history began, theologians, scholars, and truth-seekers have studied the lives of the saints. Their conclusions have ranged from the assurance that saints were spokesmen for God to the notion that saints were fanatics. Sainthood is sometimes determined in an outward manner, based upon such things as martyrdom, and various miracles of healing. This does little, however, to reflect that a man has risen from worldly consciousness to spiritual consciousness, or that the saint possesses a character "Softer than the flower, where kindness is concerned; stronger than the thunder, where principles are at stake."[*] Indeed, we look to the saints for their character rather than their miracles. Wasn't Christ on the cross portraying the greatest human character ever exhibited, (his mighty miracle of love,[†]) in forgiving those who unjustly crucified him, crushed a crown of thorns on his head, spat on him, lashed him forty times with barbed whips, and jabbed a spear into his side? Imagine the character of a man who endured such terrible cruelties and still had enough life in him to utter, "Father, forgive them for they know not what they do."[‡] By his tremendous character-qualities of love and forgiveness, turning the other cheek, reminding his disciples to "Love ye one another...,"

---

[*]Sri Yukteswarji's Vedic definition of a man of God, from the chapter entitled, "Years in my Master's Hermitage" in the *Autobiography of a Yogi*.

[†]From Paramahansa Yogananda's Christmas message of December 23, 1950 at Mount Washington.

[‡]Luke 23:34.

Jesus proved categorically that he was one of the great prophets of all time.

It would seem that if we could detect in human nature a person who had this same strength and love, plus knowledge of God, then we would be truly blessed and be within the purview of a Divine Personage. It was my great fortune and blessing to encounter such a man, who, without a shadow of a doubt, manifested the aforementioned qualities. Not only were these qualities evident to some extent to those who were close enough to him to detect them, but an even greater indication of sainthood manifested itself when he received an inner sanction to display tremendous powers. I know, I saw them first hand.

In the Indian culture, saints are deemed to have the power to uplift and to bless through their presence. One receives their blessing merely by coming within the range of their magnetism; the Hindus call this blessing a darshan. The darshan and spiritual initiation Dr. Lewis received from the young Swami Yogananda* in 1920 immediately awakened states of spiritual consciousness that had been lying dormant, waiting for that special day when his Guru would re-establish the never-severed link. The first meeting (in this incarnation) between the Guru and his great disciple established the beginning of a life-long bond and set the young man's course toward spiritual attainment rather than worldly accomplishment.

What an unlikely beginning for a saint! Dr. Lewis was born in New England and was raised in the very conservative environment, established 300 years before by the Puritans and the Pilgrims. And although the extreme righteousness and morality of the early settlers was, in a way, a good environment for spiritual living, the restrictive codes of the New Englanders allowed little latitude for truthseekers, men who would seek the counsel of a swami from India rather than an established Christian minister.

---

*Later given the title of Paramahansa by Swami Sri Yukteswarji.

Paramahansa Yogananda, one of the greatest yogis who ever lived, drew to himself various disciples, when he landed in Boston in 1920. One of these disciples was Dr. Minott W. Lewis, a married man with two children. Dr. Lewis had pursued truth in his orthodox Christian church, but it had not satisfied him, not at all. Subsequent to his baptism into Kriya Yoga and his visions of the "things of Spirit" within, Dr. Lewis asked Yogananda, "Why can't these ministers tell or show me something of these eternal truths?" Yogananda replied succinctly with the words of Jesus: "Can the blind lead the blind? Shall they both not fall into the ditch?"[*]

During Paramahansa Yogananda's first three years in America, he spent much time in New England, living for long periods with the Lewis family. When the Master finally came to the point in his ministry in which he knew it was God's will that he expand the limits of his teachings, he told Doctor that he must go west.[†] With the great security and upliftment one feels in the presence of a yogi who is One with God, Doctor Lewis wanted to go with him rather than be left to his own devices. The Master, however, told him that he must stay in Boston, continue his practice, and raise his family.

Doctor continued to press in his request until the Guru told him, "That Light which you see is greater than I am; that is God Himself!" (The Master showed Doctor Lewis this Light on Christmas Eve, 1920.[‡]) I once asked Doctor Lewis how long it took him to see that Light at will, and he replied, "It never left me." The ring of gold, surrounding a field of supernal blue light with a five-point, palpitating silver star in the center is the "Door of Heaven, by which we all pass through," as Doctor Lewis wrote in a poem.[§]

---

[*]Luke 6:39.

[†]Self-Realization Fellowship was formerly founded as a non-profit church at Mount Washington in Los Angeles in 1925.

[‡]In the next few chapters, Doctor and Mrs. Lewis share in their own words the story of that immortal night.

[§]Practices required to see this Light, which I might add, take great dint

However, even in his high state of realization, Dr. Lewis had not reached the point in his sadhana where he absolutely knew the significance of that Light. It is axiomatic that the Guru's words shattered the last vestige of ignorance about the inner perception of his disciple and catapulted him toward Spirit.

No one would ever have suspected back in the early 1920's that this young New Englander was a saint in the making, for his beginnings were similar to any other young Bostonian: attending school, obtaining a degree (in dentistry), marrying, and becoming the father of a son and daughter. It was in those inchoate years that his desire for truth was driving him, nagging him, to find out what life was all about. He wanted answers to: "Where have I come from? Why am I here? Where am I going?" God Himself answered these longing pleas when He responded through the voice and activity of Paramahansa Yogananda on Christmas Eve, 1920.

The Guru told the young dentist that all he would ever want, he would find in God. But he warned the doctor that the discipline was severe and that his former life "was over." While alluding to the new life in spirit he would lead, the master added that the rewards were beyond human comprehension, for the soul afire with the Great Light and Love of the Infinite could stand anything the world could concoct to test him.

The Guru's instructions were simple, but not easy. Dr. Lewis knew of the extreme righteousness and morality base, which is the benchmark for the initiation into any spiritual search; but he did not know that the techniques,* which the Guru would give him, would be the "Keys to the Kingdom." These techniques would accelerate his spiritual evolution, awaken his kundalini—without which no perceptible

---

of spiritual effort, are taught by Self-Realization Fellowship.

*Doctor Lewis would describe Kriya Yoga as the fastest spiritual accelerator.

spiritual growth is possible—and, most of all, lead to the quieting of his mind, which is the technical goal of yoga practice.*

The Guru's emphasis, however, was on meditation, for if there were any character flaws in a disciple, the successful practice of meditation would soon correct them.† The practice of meditation as a science has been lost in the forest of theology, but if one looks for signs of its importance, they can be found. Christ simply said, "Behold, the Kingdom of Heaven is within you."‡ Mohammed was purported to have meditated in a cave near Mecca for six months before he founded the Islamic faith. Buddha vowed to meditate under the banyan tree until the flesh would no longer cleave to his bones, if that is what it took to find Nirvana.§

The Hindu scriptures, particularly the Bhagavad Gita, not only refer many times to the practice of meditation, but also delineate instructions on how to practice it. Lesser saints, if they can be called that, such as Omar Khayyam, Zoroaster, Brother Lawrence, and Thomas à Kempis, have spoken of meditation and its value. Brother Lawrence said simply, "Look for Him within and nowhere else."

This practice of meditation was not new to Dr. Lewis, for he had been meditating before he met his Master, his soul's intuition prompting him to the practice. Doctor once told me that before he met his Guru, he used to see a light at the periphery of his consciousness. After baptism by Swami Yogananda, however, it was as if a curtain had been raised, and he began to see "signs and wonders." From that time onward there was no darkness in his meditation.

He soon found that his experiences tallied with other

---

*"Be still and know that I am God!" — Psalms 46:10.

†God's great consciousness flowing into a yogi dislodges tendencies toward anger, lust, excitement, restlessness, attachment and desire.

‡Luke 17:21.

§Nirvana is sometimes incorrectly described as "nothingness"—but it is correctly defined as the annihilation of the mind so that the Spirit can shine through.

saints—those few who recorded what they saw behind the darkness of closed eyes. Like all other saints, Dr. Lewis was tested to the very limit of his tolerance with physical pain, persecution, and, ultimately, psychological crucifixion. But he was equal to the occasion, for his love of God showed brightly above all outward trials; in the deep reverie of his meditations he was able to realize that those "little tests" meant nothing compared to the great blessings God had bestowed on him.

To dispel the myth that everyone was meditating when they came to Self-Realization to try to master this most difficult of sciences, Doctor Lewis used to tell truthseekers that there were two kinds of meditators: those who had contact with God and those who didn't. He explained that those who didn't were garnering great, good karma for making the effort to succeed by following a true instrument of God, Paramahansa Yogananda, and also gleaning a little happiness from quieting the mind. But those who contacted the Presence of God were electrified by His Presence and charged with His consciousness and energy. The darkness and delusion of incarnations was done away with by the power of God flowing through them. Psychological aberrations such as lust and anger were dislodged by God's power, never again to distract the yogi who was bent on God Realization. But most of all the yogi who attains contact with God feels a supernatural Bliss that no worldly happiness can in any way approximate. It is this Bliss and its happiness that age after age the great yogis seek. Dr. Lewis had achieved that goal.

As Dr. Lewis continued his upward climb toward spiritual liberation, those close to him saw a great change come over him. His spirituality escalated at such a pace that his wife suggested that he speak in terms that the parishioners could more easily understand. Dr. Lewis replied with kindness, "They will have to reach." It is little wonder that Paramahansa Yogananda said, "When you understand a

Foreword xvii

saint (or even recognize one), you will be one."

Doctor's very spiritual wife reflected in silence toward the end of his life, "What are you, anyway?" Mrs. Lewis herself was no ordinary mortal. She was perhaps the most righteous and moral individual who ever trod this earth, and Paramahansa Yogananda deemed her one of the smartest women he had ever known. Many devotees (even her husband) relied on her super-human psychological strength. Dr. Lewis confided in me that she was very spiritually advanced.

Others became aware of Doctor's tremendous powers as he told them in detail of their past and gave them hints about the future. Many of these hints in the lives of devotees came true in the fullness of the yogi's prediction.

Doctor would spend long hours after the Sunday service counseling the many truthseekers who came to him for guidance. Not knowing the spiritual status of Doctor, a great deal of the counseling concerned family, financial, and health matters. Few sensed that by looking beyond the temporary problems of life (which never end), this great yogi could have told them how to race quickly to the Infinite.*

During one of my Sunday afternoon interviews with Doctor, I discussed some of the devotees with whom I was meditating and serving at Hollywood Church. I had noticed that lately there had been a significant number of marriages among my former single devotee men friends. Because of this I spoke disparagingly about the women involved who were taking those men from the path to God. I presume that there was too much negativity in my voice, for Doctor spoke firmly to me: "You shouldn't speak that way about women; there is one in your future!" Being single and contemplating the monastic life, these words came as a shock

---

*When giving spiritual counsel, he would oft times open up the *Autobiography of a Yogi* and point out an eternal truth that would elude an uninitiated person. As if I were a truant child, he told me that this earth was not my true home.

to me, and I reacted emotionally, but wordlessly, toward Doctor. Then he looked at me and said, "That's all I can tell you, John." Three years after his death I was married.

It was indeed awesome to be in his presence and receive his blessing, and then have him tell you something that was lurking in the deep recesses of your brain about a spiritual misadventure, or an action that you had done that was not good for your spiritual life. He would speak strongly on such occasions with such words as, "Why do you doubt the Presence of God within you?" On occasion he would also tell me something about the practice of yoga. Many of these things were not written down, and can never be, for they can only be transmitted from yogi to yogi.

Countless truth seekers travel to India with the hope of finding a God-Realized saint or a fully illumined Guru, but such souls are rare in any land in any age. Paramahansa Yogananda said that he tromped his legs off from Point Cormerin to the Himalayas, trying to find a Guru who would slake his spiritual thirst. It was only when he met Sri Yukteswarji (who many consider the wisest yogi of all time) that his heart was satisfied. Yogananda said that he sensed his Guru knew God and could lead him to Him. It was with this same sense that I found in Dr. Lewis a soul whose spiritual attainment was beyond human comprehension (these are the same words Sri Yukteswarji used when describing the Great Babaji). Babaji's spiritual state is described further by Sri Yukteswarji: "The dwarfed vision of men cannot pierce to his transcendental star. One attempts in vain even to picture the avatar's attainment. It is inconceivable."[*]

Dr. Lewis' spiritual state was likewise inconceivable. Few had any idea of his spiritual achievement. And most treated him just like anyone else. In all walks of life, it usually takes a peer person to recognize the true genius of a

---

[*]From the chapter entitled, "Babaji, Yogi-Christ of Modern India" in the *Autobiography of a Yogi*.

musician, an artist, a scientist, etc. It would seem that the same laws for diagnosing human qualities would be even more relevant when it comes to identifying a saint. And as we have said, there is a state beyond ordinary character values that separates a saint from a sinner: his/her state of consciousness. When the truthseekers become sensitive to consciousness, then there is no question about the state of the person at interest. One begins to feel something around oneself that he/she feels around no one else: a tremendous buoyancy, an upliftment, a happiness, a state of consciousness that is beyond the ability of words to describe, for there is nothing in outward consciousness with which it can be compared.

In their teachings, the true men of God go beyond ordinary scriptural references and plumb the eternal truths of God. The sutras described in Sri Yukteswarji's *Holy Science* are example of truths not heretofore broached in this yuga. But perhaps the most vital truths of yoga have been uttered by men who have gone beyond the pale of scriptural injunctions and have penetrated to the very core of reality. Few know what the spiritual eye is—although it is represented on the images of Krishna and Buddha throughout the world—and fewer still have ever seen it, much less penetrated it. Doctor Lewis spoke in terms beyond the mind and intellect when he described what it was like to penetrate the spiritual eye. He described visions beyond the spiritual eye where the "sun of righteousness" rises, and one realizes at last (after many incarnations) that he is One with God.

One Christmas meditation at Mount Washington during the Master's time (Paramahansa Yogananda), Doctor Lewis was scheduled to assist in leading the meditation. When the time arrived for the meditation to begin, Doctor's back was giving him real pain: he was flat on the floor, unable to move. He told Master that he had done his best to shake it off, but he could not do it. Paramahansa Yogananda told him he must. And so Doctor went downstairs and took part in the meditation. Doctor told me that during that meditation, a great Spiritual Eye came to him, so expanded that he could easily penetrate through it and look on "the other side." He did so, and witnessed countless souls coming and going from the astral world. The first-hand account he gave was so vibrant with truth that it had a lasting effect on me, particularly as it brought home the short tenure of earthly life and the eternal nature of Spiritual Consciousness.

Penetration of the spiritual eye brings to the yogi great spiritual powers, not the least of which is the ability to transmit spiritual consciousness—a feat that can only be accomplished when the transmitter has penetrated the little star in the center of that light. On more than one occasion Dr. Lewis was observed blessing monks by this method and causing the disciple to wilt and fall from the great power that the yogi caused to flow through them.

Dr. Lewis often reminded the writer that he "spoke from the Light" and to listen to everything he said. Such was the abundance of Bliss that saturated Dr. Lewis during some services that he would listen to the lecture on a tape recorder after the service, for there was nothing operating in his physical body to recall the words that he had spoken from a greater consciousness.

God has been talked about by ministers from time immemorial, but the most profound blessing comes when the truthseeker has realized God—not merely studied the teachings of the Great Ones. Doctor Lewis often spoke of the tremendous truths uttered by his Guru and the param-Gurus of the Self-Realization path, but he would also counsel devotees that God could not be known through the mind or the intellect but only through the intuition of the soul. As an example, Doctor taught that Swami Sri Yukteswarji's profound treatise on the parallel truths of Hinduism and Christianity (*The Holy Science*) could only be understood by realization, and he concluded, "It took me thirty years to understand it."

Once the truthseeker has realized God, then all within the range of his magnetism are uplifted, for the vibration is high, and its residual effects remain in the place where he communed with God.* It is the paramount reason why devotees should go to Holy Places where saints and yogis have communed with God as a vital, living reality.

On one occasion when the writer was having difficulty with a certain discipline, Dr. Lewis commented, "I did it. That's why I am free." Those simple words revealed that he had finally reached the goal of all human incarnation, Oneness with God. Salvation had come perhaps eons ago, but that is a long way from final liberation in God: a state where there is at last no separation between the yogi's consciousness and God's consciousness; a state where the yogi feels the Presence of God all the time; a state where the yogi views the world as a vast dream of God and finds that there is nothing but bliss in his consciousness—all the pain, suffering, and worry of worldly life are gone, along with the attachments and desires that created the separation.

Some thirty years after Doctor's first meeting with Paramahansa Yogananda, the great guru entered mahasamadhi. That night a heavy rain fell on Los Angeles; it was very dark and stormy—somewhat reminiscent of Jesus' death, when the earth became dark and quaked. As you can imagine, those close to the Guru were very shaken at his death. Devotees were driven into worship and meditation by their grief. But God does not deny those drawn to His pure instrument, and so He appeared as the Guru to several while they were deep in their reveries. Doctor knew of these visions and wondered why he, having known the Guru more intimately and longer than any of the rest, was deprived of the Master's vision. Nevertheless, he continued his meditations. One night while deep in meditation, a great Light filled his inner forehead. Doctor was taken aback by Its bril-

---

*This refers to a statement made by Paramahansa Yogananda.

liance, until he heard a voice, soft like murmuring clouds, which spoke from within that Light and said, "It was I who came to you as your beloved Master."*

During Doctor's years in California, he lived at Encinitas Colony (part of Self-Realization Fellowship). As Vice-President of the Fellowship, he carried a very heavy load, including conducting seven services a week, carrying on administrative duties of the Colony where he was in charge, and spending long hours in counseling all those who sought his aid. Once a week he would drive to the SRF Hollywood Church and conduct a class for the monks, as well as a meditation service for the lay disciples. But all yogis must find time to be alone with God. With his busy schedule, it was all the more important for Doctor. Subsequently, he and Mrs. Lewis purchased the desert retreat house of former opera star Amelita Galli-Curci in Borrego Springs.

It was only a small desert house with a little bedroom, kitchen, bath and living room. Doctor relished the thought of being in such a quiet place with time to pursue his goals in Spirit. He would leave on Monday night or Tuesday morning from Encinitas and return on Thursday for the evening service at the Colony. During those mid-week periods, he meditated for uncountable hours.† It was there, on a balmy summer night, where Doctor beheld a great astral rainbow of many hues, spreading in supernal grandeur across the Southern Mojave Desert. Cameo-like, the faces of the Gurus appeared within the lambent light.

The Borrego Springs desert often reaches temperatures of 115 degrees; during the summer months it has the questionably unique distinction of being the hottest spot in the

---

*This reveals one of the most vital truths in the Guru-disciple relationship; that is, to advance on the spiritual path, one must realize that the Guru is none other than God Himself.

†Since his experience at Plum Island where he meditated for five hours on the rocks with the Master Paramahansa Yogananda, all restlessness had been purged from his consciousness, and he could spend as much time as he wanted in meditation.

country. In the little room where he meditated, the windows were covered with a heavy black cloth so that no light could shaft in.* Doctor would sit up at the head of his bed, propped up by pillows, and, sitting cross-legged, would meditate for hours. Mrs. Lewis would leave the little house during the day and let him be alone with God. To him, the oppressive heat was never a factor, for in his state of realization, he escaped beyond all traces of body consciousness. When he returned to Encinitas, disciples would say that they heard it had been very hot on the desert. Doctor would reply that he didn't notice it. He enjoyed his stay there—not once did he even allude to the heat of Borrego upon his return!

During a Christmas party with the monks in December of 1958 at Hollywood Church, Doctor was asked to speak and said: "Sister Daya [now known as Sri Daya Mata[†]] has asked me to relate an experience I had in the desert. On May 1, 1958, in the small hours of the morning, God showed me his Great Face." Doctor went on to say that this spiritual accomplishment took him 37 years, and that during that time he never missed his daily morning, noon, and night, meditations. This experience is incomprehensible by the intellect, for Doctor had early-on gone beyond the spiritual eye and had an experience in Cosmic Consciousness. When relating his experience in Cosmic Consciousness to me, he said, "I could see above, below, and all around me. It was the strangest thing ...." These words were uttered with humbleness and in the mildest of tones.

Nine years after Doctor's final exit from the body, Mrs. Lewis constructed a meditation chapel in Borrego by the little retreat house in honor of her husband's spiritual accomplishments. On November 1, 1969, the little chapel was dedicated by Brother Anandamoy, one of the senior broth-

---

*This was done to block out all solar light, so that the Divine Light was not diffused.
[†]President of Self-Realization Fellowship.

ers of the Self-Realization Fellowship, and a direct disciple of Paramahansa Yogananda.

Dr. Lewis said often in his lectures that when one is thus established in God, at the end of the trail, one will not even feel a ripple of fear, for the attachment to every aspect of worldly consciousness would have been severed, allowing the meditating yogi to merge consciously into the Great Light of the Infinite from which all things have come.

Towards the end of his life, he told me he no longer needed to meditate, for he felt the Presence of God all the time. I sometimes hesitate telling devotees this, lest they find an excuse not to meditate, but it must be noted that a lifetime of many hours of meditation and practicing Kriya Yoga a thousand at a time resulted in his being able to commune with God without bodily fixture.*

Dr. Lewis was always filled with energy and happiness; indicative of his constant state of God communion, the yogi communes with God without bodily fixation, waking or sleeping. He was the pre-eminent minister in Self-Realization churches from 1953–1960. His lectures were conducted mostly in the San Diego Temple (then called a church). The complete description of the great yogi's final exit from the body is described by Mrs. Mildred Lewis in the Self-Realization memorial booklet dedicated to Dr. Lewis, *The Life Story of Dr. M. W. Lewis.*†

John Rosser
March 26, 1991

---

*Those who knew Doctor, know he was never boastful; publicly he never would have said this about himself. When John Rosser exclaimed he had a wonderful meditation, while sitting on the pulpit at Hollywood Church where Doctor Lewis was speaking, Dr. Lewis replied softly: "You were near the instrument."

†Interestingly enough, the manner of Doctor Lewis' exit was foretold by Paramahansa Yogananda in a letter written from Encinitas in 1945 (contained in this volume), "You will be consciously ushered out of body by Guru [referring to Swami Sri Yukteswar]. You have earned it by all these years of Kriya Yoga practice." — The Editor

Treasures Against Time

Mildred Lewis, 1916

Mrs. Lewis arriving in Los Angeles, 1980

Chapter 1

Mildred Lewis Reminisces

As Doctor Lewis was going to lunch one October day, he passed a "strange-looking man" crossing the street. Doctor Lewis remembered this incident because the fast-moving figure, dressed in an orange-colored coat and turban, distinctly stood out.[*] Doctor later recalled his first glimpse of Swami Yogananda, "After we passed each other, I turned around and looked at him, and he turned around and looked at me." Almost two months later, an opportunity for Doctor to meet this Swami presented itself, as the following story will tell.[†]

Mildred Lewis Meets Swami Yogananda

Before Swami Yogananda came to America, Doctor and I had joined the Rosicrucian Society, as Doctor had for some years been searching for greater enlightenment. It was the custom of the Society to have lectures on Sunday evenings. One Sunday, a very rainy night in November 1920, I invited a friend to go to the Sunday Evening lecture held in Boston. We rode into the city on the street car and subway.

---

[*]Boston was fairly conservative at this time in 1920.
[†]Doctor Lewis was affectionately known as Doctor. The stories in this chapter were compiled and edited from a number of diaries and journals kept by Mildred Lewis. Sometimes Mrs. Lewis referred to herself indirectly as "Mrs. Lewis," and at other times she wrote in first person. — The Editor

When we arrived at the lecture hall, the leader in charge, a Mrs. Clemens of the Society, met me at the door. "Mrs. Lewis," she said, "after the lecture is over, I want to introduce you to an Indian Swami who is attending the lecture." I remember looking around to see an Indian gentleman, but I did not see one, as the lecture hall was rather dimly lit except for the platform.

When the lecture was over, my friend and I went to the reception room to wait. Shortly thereafter, Mrs. Clemens appeared with a dark-skinned, Indian Swami whose long black hair flowed over his shoulders. He was wearing an orange turban, orange coat, puttees, and sort of orange-colored, high-laced shoes. I was not accustomed to seeing anyone dressed this way; I must have been a strange-looking person to this Hindu Swami, as he was for me. Mrs. Clemens then introduced me to this Oriental—a Swami Yogananda Giri of Calcutta, India. As I look back on this meeting, I was no doubt so awe-struck as to be speechless. I had very little to say, but I have never forgotten this meeting.

When I reached home, I immediately told Doctor about it, and his curiosity was aroused. We talked of it often. Within the week Doctor came home from the office and said, who should be approaching him, but this same East Indian; Doctor told me, "I think the swami that you met walked by my office today."

Sister Yogamata Meets Swami Yogananda

Shortly after the swami passed near Doctor's office, the following event took place. Mrs. Alice Hasey, who later became Sister Yogamata, was arranging flowers one Sunday morning in the West Somerville Unitarian Church. As she was working with the flowers, she glanced down the auditorium and saw an East Indian sitting in one of the church pews.

She approached him and inquired, "Is there anything I can do for you?" He thanked her and explained that the minister had invited him to visit. Now, Swami Yogananda had been staying in Boston, after attending the Congress of Religious Liberals, the purpose of which, on the surface, appeared to be his reason for coming to America. After the Sunday service, Mrs. Hasey met briefly with Swami Yogananda. She invited him to her home at 9 Lester Terrace [West Somerville, Massachusetts] to meet with a group of her lady friends who read and discussed metaphysical books.

It was not long after this that Mrs. Hasey called her dear friend—Doctor Lewis—on the telephone and told him about a certain Hindu Swami whom she had met and who had talked with her friends. She told Doctor that he *must* meet this Swami Yogananda. Doctor was skeptical, but, nevertheless, he asked her right away to make an appointment for him. The appointment was made for Christmas Eve at Unity House, Park Square, Boston.

Doctor Meets Swami Yogananda

When Doctor met Swami Yogananda he was very skeptical, for he had had much warning from his parents and friends not to be fooled or misled by charlatans in the name of religion. Doctor began by asking many questions; and the Master gave him satisfying answers. Doctor said, "It says in the Bible, 'If thine eye be single, thy whole body shall be full of Light.'* Can you tell me anything about this?" Master said, "I think so." Doctor then said, "I have asked many, but no one seems to know about it." Swamiji said to Doctor, "Can the blind lead the blind? They both fall into the same ditch."† Whereupon Doctor in his great enthusiasm said, "For heaven's sake, please show me."

Master then looked right into Doctor's eyes and asked, "Will you always love me as I love you?" Doctor replied that he would and Master said, "I take charge of your life."

---

*Matthew 6:22.
†Luke 6:39.

Master then placed a tiger skin on the floor of his room—and asked Doctor to sit cross-legged on it; he sat down opposite him. Then Master showed him the Light: Doctor saw the star in the spiritual eye and the thousand-petaled lotus.

Doctor often has said, over these many years of discipline, little did he realize [at the time just] what those words meant, and also [little did he realize] what the admonition of Master meant when he said, "I want you to promise that you will never avoid me." This Doctor did promise to do, but many times it was very difficult, for the discipline of a guru is not an easy path, but it is always for the disciple's own good in guiding him to the one Abode of Light.

After describing Doctor's meeting with Master at Unity House, I should write at this point about "the rolling pin incident."

God's Light and the Rolling Pin

It was our custom to dress the Christmas tree on Christmas Eve so that it was a complete surprise the next morning for our children Bradford and Brenda. Doctor's appointment with the swami was Christmas Eve, so when Doctor left the house, he told me he would be back in time to do the tree. He left thinking he would be gone just a short time, but it was many, many hours later when he returned. I knew nothing about where he was going. He just said, "I will be back in a little while, and we will trim the Christmas tree." I remember his instructions to have everything ready.*

As the evening progressed, everything was ready, but there was no Father to put up the tree! I tried to fix the tree in a wooden box as we used to do before you could purchase metal stands. It was no use: the Christmas tree just would not stay upright in that box. So I gave up the idea and kept thinking Doctor would soon come home.

---
*In the next chapter, Doctor Lewis tells this story in his own words.

Hour after hour passed, and before long it was midnight. I was getting upset, for how were we going to get the tree ready for Santa Claus before the children came running downstairs? Now I was really going to do something about this Christmas tree business, and so I prepared myself. There was a rocking chair in the kitchen, and I planted myself in it, sweater sleeves rolled up, with a rolling pin firmly clutched in my right hand. There I sat. As the clock neared one o'clock, I first heard the automobile come into the driveway, then the garage doors closed, the door opened, and soon the footsteps came from the back hall into the kitchen. I was truly ready to swing that rolling pin!

Doctor came in the kitchen with this divine smile on his face—pleasant as could be—with the glow of being with Master, and so I could not touch him. I dropped the rolling pin. There were words, but that was all. The tree was put up and trimmed, and Santa Claus arrived before the children awoke. This is the story that Master used to tell from the lecture platform. Moral: When you are in God's Light, nothing (not even a wrathful wife's rolling pin!) can touch you. Doctor always said this was his first real Christmas.

Mildred Lewis Becomes a Disciple

Well, Christmas came and went. Soon after New Year's we had an invitation to dinner at Mrs. Hasey's home. We arrived at her house—a cold winter's night—and took off our wraps in the hallway. Then I was escorted into the parlor, and right in front of me sat Swami Yogananda. This was most upsetting: Doctor and Mrs. Hasey had planned this meeting without my knowledge. After the rolling pin incident, I had said I was not going to get messed up with any religion—and no Hindu!

[Shortly thereafter Swami Yogananda called Mrs. Lewis into another room, where they had a private meeting. Years later she would explain that a veil had been drawn over her consciousness about that meeting; nevertheless, it was clear that the swami changed her consciousness during their meeting. And as Doctor Lewis recounts in the following chapter, her loyalty and devotion did not waver from that point on. — The Editor]

In June of 1921, at the end of the season, we held our first picnic at Lexington Park on a Sunday afternoon. All of the members who had been attending the meetings in Boston and at Sister Yogamata's home were present. When the gathering was over, Master came to me, "I would like to talk with you. Will you come to Sister's home tomorrow afternoon?" I went, and that was when Master really accepted me as a disciple. All sins were forgiven, as he told Doctor in 1920 Christmas Eve. I had during the ensuing years many illnesses—not too serious—but, nevertheless, my health at times was not all that good. Master always told me, "What you are suffering now is not of this life, but of former lives."

The Three Tea Leaves

The story of the three tea leaves was my first realization of the supernatural powers of Swami Yogananda. In 1921, as I became more and more acquainted with Master, I would talk with him if anything unusual happened in regards to the health of my two children, Brad and Brenda. It was rather a common incident in Bradford's daily life to complain of a stomach-ache, not necessarily after eating.

One day he was complaining and complaining. And so I thought, I am going to call Swamiji on the telephone; he was staying in Boston at this time. I asked him what he could advise me to do for Bradford. This is what he told me to do: Take three tea leaves and put them in a cup. Take a slight pinch of sugar and put it on the tea leaves. Pour on the tea leaves a half a cup of hot water. When the tea is steeped, after a few minutes give him a teaspoonful of this brew and continue giving it to him until the stomach-ache is gone.

I did just exactly what he told me to do, and the child had no more stomach-aches. This to me was a miracle of healing; and I believe, from this time on, my faith was established in Master's spiritual powers. I know, and we all know: it wasn't the three tea leaves!

The Drive Around Mystic Lake Parkway

One evening on a warm night in June 1921, Master asked Doctor to take him to a beautiful park area around the Mystic Lakes. The gardens each spring would be filled with beautiful flowers. Doctor told Mrs. Lewis that during their ride around the park, Swamiji had asked Doctor to stop the car. Twilight was descending at this time. Swamiji got out of the car and ran across an area of new grassland towards a beautiful flower garden.

Doctor could not believe his eyes. Swamiji was picking flowers as fast as he could and came back to the car with arms full of various blossoms. When Swamiji got into the car, he said, "I picked the flowers for you, Doctor." Doctor thanked him and then got out of the area quickly—for fear that the Park Police would be after them. Later on, Doctor explained to Swamiji that in the state parks of Massachusetts, one isn't allowed to pick flowers.

The Boarding House: Winter, 1921

Before Master spent any time with Mrs. Hasey or Doctor and me, he lived in a boarding house on a street running out of Harvard Square, Cambridge. There were several Hindu students living in this boarding house. One night Master asked Doctor to come to this house and have curry with the students. While eating the curry Master said to Doctor, "It's pretty hot." Doctor agreed!

Another occasion in the Winter of 1921, Doctor—for some reason—wanted to get a message to Swamiji. While I went and delivered the message, Doctor sent his nurse to the house to stay with our children. It was bitter cold around zero. I had to walk some distance to the streetcar; and at the stop of the streetcar, there was a candy shop. I went in and bought a box of chocolates. Arriving at the address of the boarding house, I rang the doorbell, hoping to be asked to enter. A heavy woman came to the door, and I asked if I could speak with the swami. She closed the door, and I stood in the freezing weather waiting for the swami to appear. Finally it happened; he opened the door. I gave him the written message from Doctor and passed him the box of candy. What transpired at that time! Master's eyes were full of tears. I was completely dismayed and returned right home. What prompted me to take a gift to the swami? I had never known one always takes a gift to the Guru.

Organs, Limeade, and Tasty Indian Food

Several months before we were married, Minie was interested in buying an Estey Organ. These organs had an electric pump attached to the right side of the organ, boxed in such a way as it was not at all unsightly. Minie finally decided on the model he liked (at the time). After we moved into our new home, it was delivered—a two-manual, full foot-pedaled organ in a golden oak case.

At 19 Whitman Street, we had a living room, den, dining room, kitchen, three bedrooms, and a bath. We had our furniture all selected and paid for; a ceraceous walnut bedroom suite was given to us by my Mother and Father. I made all the curtains of scrim, hemstitching them by hand. We lived in this house for a year and three months, and decided it was too big. A small two-apartment house was being built next door by Grandpa Lewis, and so we swapped houses. Bradford was just 7 months old. In this house at 23 Whitman Street, we had one bedroom and a den. We were certainly short-sighted, for in April, 1919, Brenda was born, then we were cramped for room.

When Bren was three months old, we bought the house immediately in back of us at 24 Electric Avenue, where we had three bedrooms, two baths, and a wonderful playroom for the children. This is the house that Master liked so much. Here we had a large kitchen well supplied with appliances—a large stove, sink, and pantry. How many Hindu dinners came out of this kitchen to serve the many Hindu friends of Master! This was the house that had a lovely back porch, where Master and Doctor would sit on warm evenings and drink Master's limeade. We stayed in this house from June, 1919, to November, 1926.

The big problem when we moved from 19 to 23 Whitman Street was moving the Estey organ. After the carpenters were consulted, it was decided to move the organ across a bridge [on the second story] between the two houses. This took place on a cold day in January. It was accomplished, but what a hazardous piece of work!

For the next move, the oak organ was sold. A larger mahogany model was purchased and delivered directly from the Estey Company to 24 Electric Avenue. In this house we had much more room for the organ. When Master was with us, he loved to play this organ. He would open all the stops. I think his favorite chant was "None Can Tone Me." I often would say, "We will have to move, if you play so loud." With the windows closed, you could hear the organ a block away!

On the bedroom level, there was a beautiful white tile bathroom. Using a circular shower curtain, one took a shower in the tub. What an attraction for Master! As such a facility would have been unknown in India, I can now understand how Master loved this shower and bathroom. After his daily morning shower, I would attempt to clean up. Water was everywhere, and towels were loaded with water. Being inexperienced in marriage, I was certainly easily discouraged about how easy it was to keep the home clean.

After this daily bath, Master would come downstairs all enthusiastic about cooking some tasty Indian dish for Doctor's lunch. Then, in the afternoon, we would start cooking for the evening meal, very often serving guests dinner. After the evening meal, Doctor and any guests would sit around the table until the wee hours of the morning, and Master would tell stories and discuss the Hindu scriptures. There were all sorts of discussions!

One evening we had the Wilbur Lewis Family (Doctor's older brother) and other guests to dinner. After dinner there was a telephone call for Swamiji. In this house the telephone was in the playroom, right off of the kitchen. During the dinner Wilbur, Jr., then about 6 years old, did not feel too well, so we put him on the couch in the playroom.

After the dinner we were all seated around the table—no doubt Swamiji was telling us an interesting story—when the telephone rang. The call was for Swamiji. Taking the telephone from the table at the head of the couch, Master sat down. He was talking away, when suddenly this young Wilbur cried out, "You're sitting on me." Swamiji jumped up, telephone in hand. How he laughed! He ended his conversation and then came back to the dining room to tell us about how startled he was to hear, "You're sitting on me!"

The Stanley Steamer Story

When the weather started to get warm in the Spring of 1922, Swamiji would often ask Doctor to take him to visit someone, or they would drive to the outskirts of the city and find a quiet spot to meditate under the stars. One such evening, they drove off to a nearby reservation called Middlesex Fells, a State Park in a heavily-wooded area that had an observatory. They had been there before, where they meditated at the top of this wooden structure on a hill, from which one could see the lights of the city of Boston. At this time Doctor had a Stanley Steamer: a five-passenger, auto touring car. No car ever gave a smoother ride; Master certainly did enjoy riding in the evening—especially when the weather was warm. As it was not possible to drive in this parkway, Doctor parked the car on a street nearby the entrance.

As for me, I was at home with the children. The hour was late, and I was concerned about when Master and Doctor would be home. At this time I answered a call on the telephone:

> "Medford Police Station calling, this is Lieutenant so and so. Is this Mrs. Lewis?"
>
> "Yes, sir."
>
> "Do you know where your husband is?"
>
> "No, sir."
>
> "We found his car, a Stanley Steamer, on the street near Middlesex Fells entrance. We were concerned about his leaving it there, as a group of young people were coming from a dance. We saw a pair of binoculars lying on the back seat. And so rather than have it damaged in some way, we towed the car to the Medford Police Station. When your husband contacts you, please give him this message."

The hours slipped by. I remember so well how I kept going out on the front piazza to see if I could see two foot-travelers coming up the hill. Finally in the distance I could hear trudging feet and voices. They were coming up the hill. When they got to the house, I opened the door and said nothing. We all sat down. I could see how weary they were. When I told them the Medford Police Station called about midnight (it was now after 2 A.M.) and said the car was at the station, of course, they were relieved to know it was not stolen. Poor Doctor! He had to walk five more miles to get the Stanley Steamer, with the binoculars still on the back seat.

Swamiji and I sat up and waited for Doctor to return. Doctor told us how he was cross-examined [at the police station] about his whereabouts; and we all had a good laugh over it. After a light meal, we all retired for a good night's rest.

The First Flower Ceremony

The first flower ceremony was held in June, 1922. It was held on the second floor of Mrs. Hasey's home. The members sat in the downstairs rooms meditating. Then each member would go up to a small room where Master had a little altar. At this time only the pictures of Lahiri Mahasaya and Sri Yukteswar were on the altar. A vase with beautiful white roses was also between the pictures. Directed to do so by Master, each one would kneel before the altar, take a rose, and lay it on the altar. Master was seated by the altar. Then he would bless each one of us. If only I could have known, what a privilege it is to be blessed by a great Guru.

[In later years Paramahansa Yogananda gave a pair of slippers as a Christmas gift to Mrs. Lewis. Enclosed with the slippers was a card remembering her efforts "at the First Festival or Convocation held in the Church of the Advent:"

To Mildred,

With boundless blessings, P. Yogananda

A little token given in appreciation for being the spokes-Mam of the first Satsanga festival at Boston and all that you have done to further its cause ever since.

Very sincerely yours, PY]

Mohawk Trail

During the winter months, Swamiji often talked to us about taking a trip via automobile in the Spring. So in June, 1922, we planned the famous Mohawk Trail, White Mountain trip.* We had a new R & V Knight car—Swamiji, Doctor, Mrs. Lewis, and Bradford were the passengers. Brenda stayed with Grandpa and Grandma Lewis.

We left West Somerville and drove across the state over the scenic Mohawk Trail, stopping the first night in Charlton at a guest house by the roadside. The weather was beautiful, warm and clear. How happy Swamiji was to get out in the country side! In the morning, we left Charlton and continued on the trail to North Adams, Massachusetts.

From here we headed north into Vermont, making our first stop at Bellows Falls around noon. We were equipped to cook over sterno heat, and this day we did just that. We purchased supplies in a country store and found a suitable spot by a rushing brook. Here we cooked the curry. A curry cooked out of doors is the best; and Swamiji being so happy, we enjoyed every last bite of it!

After washing all of the curry dishes in cold brook water, we left and headed for Ludlow, Vermont. On the journey to Ludlow, we encountered many, very steep hills; and on one of these Swamiji kept saying, "Go fast, Doctor." I do not recall the speed we were going down hill, but it was fast. Near the bottom of the grade, there was a noise under the hood! Something had let go. Finally Doctor stopped the auto, got out, and looked under the hood. Some part found only in a Knight motor car was damaged. There was not a chance of getting a part in the country; but fortunately, just beyond on the roadside, was a garage, to which we coasted. Doctor explained what was wrong, and the mechanic made the part. After a long wait, we went on to Ludlow, Vermont.

*Paramahansaji's poem "Mohawk Trail" refers to this trip. The poem is found in *Songs of the Soul*, published by Self-Realization Fellowship, Los Angeles.

After Ludlow, we toured through the White Mountains for a day, and then went on to Dover, New Hampshire, where my parents lived. We were expected in the early evening, but it was very much later when we arrived. Beds were all ready for us, my mother was away at Duxbury at the time, so we quieted down after awhile.

In the morning I went into the kitchen, and on the table were a huge egg and a note from my father. The egg was a double-yolked egg for my son Bradford; I cooked it for him.

When Swamiji came down for breakfast, I told him about the double-yolked egg I had cooked for Bradford's breakfast. Let me tell you! I did the wrong thing, and for the rest of Swamiji's life, he never let me forget it.

So in his later years I made it up to him. I knew where I could obtain double-yolked eggs. Each week he received two dozen from me, and I even purchased them on our last visit to Mount Washington before Master's Mahasamadhi.

The First Ashram: Waltham

Master started his lectures in Boston in the Fall of 1921 and continued through the Spring of 1922. At this time, as summer approached, Master wanted to start an ashram, or hermitage. As this was all new to the Lewises, he got Sister Yogamata to see about some place nearby, where he could get out of the city. Hardy's Pond in Waltham was chosen. Sister had some money which she put down on this property, I believe with the Moody Land Company.

Well, the property was unzoned and not specified, but this was where our Swamiji was located for his first hermitage! Of course, as there was a lack of funding, the building was rather cheaply constructed right on the bank of Hardy's Pond. It was constructed out of cement blocks without any bathroom facilities. It was rather scenic, however, for there were some beautiful trees on the land. One other thing I remember, the property consisted of the last lots at the end of the road, and so there was no one else beyond.

On Sundays we always went to Waltham, where quite a group of students assembled, and Master gave a lecture, followed by a dinner of curry. Of course, in the winter months the Waltham property had to be closed. About three or four years after the building of this hermitage, Sister Yogamata decided to have her own cottage built to the left of the Hermitage. She stayed there for some time.

No Secrets

One day, while we were visiting with Sister Yogamata in her summer home at Plum Island, Mass., the following little incident occurred one afternoon. Swamiji was resting in his room. The door was ajar, and Doctor and I eagerly awaited his awakening. As a little joke was always in order in those early days, we decided to tie a string to Swamiji's ankle, so when he started to get up, the door, being located as it was, it would slam shut. We executed our little joke so painstakingly—tiptoeing around the room, feeling sure that Swamiji was deep in sleep. After everything was completed, we viewed our project with great glee and then started to take our places to watch and listen for the big bang. Just over the transom we heard, "Ha! Ha! So you are going to tie your Swami to the door?" No secrets with our Swamiji.

The First Advertisement

The first advertisement of Yogoda Sat-Sanga occurred in 1921 or 1922, when Master wanted to advertise the little Yogoda Booklet. Master requested the reader to send ten cents, to cover postage and mailing, to our address at 24 Electric Avenue. Once in a while, a letter would come with a request for the booklet. The mailing was then prepared from our dining room table. From time to time Master would call on the telephone to inquire if any letters had come. The letters came in very slowly, but it was the beginning of the snowball which Master had always predicted would come.

About this same time, Master decided to see me once every week. So I got a young woman to come every Saturday morning to care for the children, and I went to Mrs. Hasey's house (Sister's), where Master would counsel me. He would talk to me about my behavior and the general discipline which I needed; and then we would meditate.

"Sit down, Swamiji"

It was Swamiji's custom to spend four or five days of each week at our home, 24 Electric Avenue, West Somerville, Massachusetts. On one of these occasions, the day started out to involve a lot of cooking. Various kinds of curries were being prepared for the evening meal. During this particular afternoon, Bradford, who was three years old, was getting more mischievous by the minute. After trying many times to quiet him, so we could go on with the cooking, I decided to put him upstairs in his crib. This was not what he wanted! Repeatedly he would come downstairs, and repeatedly I would take him upstairs.

Swamiji could see that with all these interruptions, no curries would be completed. So, as he was shelling peas at the time, he took a basket of peas up to the bedroom and sat by the crib to watch Bradford—and, incidentally, to keep him in the crib. Soon the crying started; such howls from the bedroom! Bradford would start climbing out; and Swamiji would put him back. After many minutes of this procedure, Bradford promised he would be good, so Swamiji came downstairs with Bradford following—still sobbing and red-eyed from this long period of discipline.

Swamiji resumed his cooking; and Bradford watched him for some time. Before long Bradford started pulling a kitchen chair—dragging it close to the kitchen range—to where Swamiji was standing. The next thing we knew,

Bradford said, "Sit down, Swamiji!" Swamiji often told this story: "Though the child was unhappy with his punishment, yet he was disciplined by love."

The Years Speed By

Master kept pushing on. The first out-of-town lecture series he gave was in Worcester, Massachusetts, at the Bancroft Hotel, for five nights. The last night Doctor took me to the lecture; it meant driving fifty miles to Worcester and returning, and that was not an easy drive in the early twenties. After the lecture, I remember, we had a light supper and then headed for Boston. After we were on our way, Master announced he wanted to have a lecture series in New York. Of course, we were not happy to have Master leaving us. As he began to explain his plans, a blow came I will never forget: "Doctor, I will have to have a thousand dollars." We had two babies and had just bought a house and a Franklin automobile. I was completely upset by this, but that was the way it went. Master got it; and so he went off to New York with Sister and two or three other students who had been attending the lectures in Boston.

Doctor and I did not attend this set of lectures; but later on, Master returned to New York and had another successful lecture course. Doctor and I later went to New York and attended some of these classes. We stayed at the old Waldorf Astoria Hotel for a week-end. After this, Master stayed at the Hotel Pennsylvania; two other times we also stayed there.

Of course, during this time Master was busy traveling to many cities, but for a few years he always spent every Christmas with us. How eagerly we awaited his arrival at Christmas time! After Mount Washington was purchased, Master stayed there for the holidays. In 1926, Master wrote a letter to Doctor wherein he said, "In ten years you will spend Christmas here with me and Dolly and Roscoe."*

---

*Mr. and Mrs. Roscoe Elliott, sister and brother-in-law of Dr. Lewis.

During the next ten years we struggled on. In 1928 Master had a very successful campaign in Boston. It started in September. Classes and the formation of a group went on until the end of the year. I cannot remember whether or not Master spent the Christmas of 1928 with us.

During the eight days the lectures in Symphony Hall [Boston] were in progress, we attended them. Master insisted that Brad and Brenda also be there. Often we would go to the Copley Plaza. Then would come room service—bringing pistachio ice cream and hot chocolate sauce—such unforgettable meetings!

At each Symphony Hall lecture, there was a free will offering taken by the ushers. Sometimes the collections were pretty big. Master had Doctor, Dolly, and me look out for the money; and we would get it to the car going to the hotel. One night as we were leaving Symphony Hall, we saw two rough-looking men standing to one side of the marquee. Doctor spied them and quickly held Dolly and me back. And as he did, these men ran off, and so all was saved.

During this time Master met many influential people in Boston; whereas, in 1920, no one was interested in yoga. During this later time, Master was entertained a great deal, and had many, many speaking engagements throughout the Boston area and at the various colleges. Doctor was with Master a great deal at this time, especially accompanying him or driving him to some function.

Master stayed in Boston for some time into 1929. A good group was formed; and, in fact, two groups were formed: one was held at the home of Mr. and Mrs. Joel Goldsmith in Brookline, Massachusetts; and the other was held at 543 Boylston Street, Mrs. Clark's Studio. As usually happens, the winter came on full blast, and then the attendance began to diminish. But the meetings were always held at 543 Boylston Street. Later, some of the group wanted to go to a Hotel, and so we moved to the Statler Hotel in Park Square. These meetings continued for over a year.

At this time, Doctor and I went to California [to Mount Washington] for our August vacation. While we were away, some of the members decided to reorganize the group. Master had put Doctor in charge. But when we returned, we learned about all the changes in leadership which had been made in our absence. It was not long before this matter was straightened out, and the meetings continued, minus the people who caused the trouble! Gradually, some of those who joined this dissenting group came back to the meetings rather ashamedly.

As the years went on, it was often a struggle to keep the meetings going. The only time the meetings were not held in winter was when we had snow or ice storms and automobile travel impossible. Each June equinox we held a flower ceremony like the one Master performed in Sister Yogamata's home in 1922. This service marked the end of our meetings for the summer months.*

The Icy Road

During the years that Doctor Lewis carried on the Boston Center, he had to drive—after finishing his professional duties—from our home in Arlington, Massachusetts, to Boston, where the center was located. Often he would be pressed for time. One particular winter night, when the roads were covered with ice and snow, Doctor was accompanied by his sister, Mrs. Laura Elliott, and Sister Yogamata.

As the trio sped along, everything was seemingly going along just fine. At one point on Doctor's route, a narrow bridge rose slightly over the roadway and crossed some railroad tracks. As the group reached the road level with the narrow bridge before them, they suddenly came upon a car, spun sideways on the icy road.

The thought flashed in Doctor's mind, "Why should this happen, just when we are going to our meeting?" But then

---

*Services resumed the week after Labor Day.

it was just as if a great unseen hand had reached down and stopped their car, because their car stopped just before reaching the other car obstructing the roadway.

Knowing that God had protected them, Sister Yogamata and Mrs. Elliott were momentarily speechless. Then Sister Yogamata said, "Doctor, did you feel that great Force?" And Doctor replied, "I did, Sister, for we never could have stopped otherwise."

The Depression Years

During some of these early years we held the Self-Realization meetings in our home in Arlington, Massachusetts at 18 Field Road; in 1929, we moved to 29 Edgehill Road, also in Arlington. The meetings continued at this address until 1943, when they were conducted at the former meeting place: 543 Boylston Street, Boston. In 1945, the meetings were turned over to Mr. Arthur Smith and Mr. Bradford Lewis.

During our 1940 visit to Mount Washington at Christmas time, Master decided to take a group of us to Mount Baldy. The weather was beautiful, and there was snow on Mount Baldy. We were driving along, and rather suddenly I said, "How long before Doctor and I will come to Los Angeles?" He said, "In five years." And so it was. I had tried so many times to get an answer to that question.

Tickets to Los Angeles were difficult to come by during the war, but we were fortunate, in 1941, in being able to spend Christmas with Master. Our good fortune continued through 1945. Sometimes we would not have a confirmation of tickets until just days ahead of the time we had set aside, which was Doctor's vacation—August to Labor Day.*

─────────

*During this time Doctor and Mrs. Lewis would visit the Master twice each year: during Doctor's vacation, which took place usually in August, and at Christmas time. On February 20th, 1939, Paramahansaji wrote, "Your letter breathed an ineffable sweetness and love—our love has stood the test of time. I never can tell you how I enjoy when you come here. You both come this summer and see things moving."

The Guru's Blessing

In September of 1934, Mrs. Lewis suffered a very serious heart attack while attempting to prevent a boat from slipping off a trailer.* The doctor treating her said that she might possibly live five additional years, provided she precisely followed the regimen which the [medical] doctor prescribed. During the next five years, Mrs. Lewis was restricted in much of her physical activity, at times barely able to walk across the room.

At one point, Doctor and Mrs. Lewis visited Master at Mount Washington. One evening, Master asked Mrs. Lewis to step onto his porch—off his sitting room—where he gave her some techniques to follow (which she never divulged). He then took her two hands in his and said, "You'll be all right now." Her personal cardiac physician, a longtime friend of both Doctor and Mrs. Lewis, was aware that something had taken place, for the improvement could not have occurred under normal physical convalescence. Mrs. Lewis never talked about the illness, possibly to keep its serious nature from her children. Doctor Lewis, of course, was aware of the seriousness of it and of the healing which had occurred.

God's Instant Help

Everyone looked forward to the vacations—which Master planned—from the pressures of everyday life at Mount Washington and Encinitas. In 1939, Master took a group of devotees to the World's Fair in San Francisco. They went in several cars caravan-style. In those days, motels were not so common as they are now, and so finding accommodations at nightfall for many devotees was not always easy.

Upon reaching Santa Maria, about half-way down the coast on the San Francisco–Los Angeles Highway, the devotees were ready for a night's rest, but no facilities of any kind

---
*This story was written by Brenda Lewis.

appeared. Finally, Dr. Lewis asked Master to intercede. Master paused for a moment; through gathering darkness, he saw a light from a not-too-distant house. Master dispatched Mrs. Lewis and another devotee to go to the door. Mrs. Lewis was reluctant, arguing that no one would have accommodations for such a large group. But despite her protestations, she followed the Master's direction and approached the front door of a lovely Santa Maria house. A sweet lady answered the door, and when the problem was posed, the lady graciously offered the entire house to the traveling yogis, and said she would sleep in the back house.

On another occasion in 1949, Master and a caravan of devotees were plying their way through the mountains of middle-California, the High Sierras, highest in the nation. They arrived in Bridgeport, a town of very high altitude, very late, as it had been a long drive from Los Angeles. Again, there were no motels or hotels available. And again Doctor Lewis asked the Master to use his powers of Divine intercession. At that very moment, a car pulled alongside the lead caravan-car.

The driver asked if there was something he could do to help. Doctor Lewis responded that they needed a place to house the people in the cars. The stranger was most accommodating and pointed to a building right across from where they had stopped, a new hotel that he owned, that had not opened for business yet, but which was ready for occupancy. He invited the entire group to stay there.

Prayer on Stair Landing

Every day when Doctor Lewis went to his office in the Lewis Building in West Somerville, he would walk up one flight of stairs, where there was a landing which led to an alcove. It was his practice to stop in the alcove, practice three kriyas, and wait for the spiritual eye to appear. He never proceeded on up the stairs to his office until that light came, and he knew God was with him.

Mrs. Lewis had a similar pattern at her home on the grounds of the San Diego Temple. She had to climb a quite long stairway, where there was a landing halfway up. She climbed very slowly in later years, praying mentally OM at each step. At the landing, she rested and repeated a silent prayer before continuing on to her bedroom on the second floor.*

Enveloped in a Blue Light

In 1941, Master came to Boston with one of his disciples. We provided a very comfortable apartment for them in the Myles Standish Hotel. It was a wonderful spot for Master to meet people. They cooked their own foods; every day I would drive into town and take them fresh vegetables and fruits. It was a very happy time for all.

During Master's visit to Boston, we had a real "get-together" in South Duxbury at our summer home. Curries were prepared for this festive occasion. Mr. and Mrs. Roscoe Elliott and Mr. and Mrs. Bradford Lewis were also present.

Master, the disciple accompanying him, and Bradford all said they would go into the water. They dressed for bathing, while the rest of us stood on the porch overlooking the beach where they were going in. Such hollering and shouting as they stepped into the frigid water! Soon they all got wet and came back to the house, remarking about the cold water. Bradford said, "While I was standing in the water with Master, he was completely enveloped in a blue light." Later Doctor asked Master about this event; Master said, "I had to go completely within to overcome the cold water."

Later on in the evening, we all drove back to Boston. What a glorious day we had! Doctor Lewis and Roscoe Elliott bought the Master a Dodge sedan. Master was driven back to Washington; later, he was driven west, where he met many devotees along the way.

*This story was written by Brenda Lewis.

The Guru's Intercession

It was always exciting when Master planned to take a group of disciples to a special event. One particular night in August, some time in the early 1940's, was no exception. Master's driver parked the car under the portico at Mt. Washington; there disciples gathered as they prepared to go to Hollywood Bowl for a concert being conducted by Antonia Brico, a lady conductor.

The following morning, Doctor was to entrain for Boston, timed to arrive Monday morning in order to treat patients at his office. Now, it was not at all unusual to be waiting for Master, as he had many appointments and telephone calls; someone was always trying to get in touch with him! The disciples were quietly waiting by the car, including Doctor Lewis. As Doctor stood there, he inadvertently placed his hand on the jam of the open door; and just then Mrs. Lewis, unconsciously, perhaps in all the excitement, slammed the car door.

Doctor's three fingers up to the second joint were crushed to the actual shape of the door jamb; the pain was indescribable. Panic flashed through Mrs. Lewis' mind, for it was Doctor's right hand; and since Doctor was a dentist, their entire future would be adversely affected, if his hand were damaged beyond hope of complete recovery. In a trice, Mrs. Lewis dashed up the stairs, where she found Master, and quickly related the tragedy.

With his super-human consciousness, Master looked at her calmly and said, "Don't talk. Go back to the car and tell Doctor *not* to look at his hand. Tell him to put it inside of his coat." Doctor immediately obeyed. Master said there would be no delay, and so they all departed immediately for the Hollywood Bowl Concert.

Years later, Doctor told a disciple that he was perfectly willing to keep his hand inside of his coat and to follow Master's directions, for as long as he did so, he felt no pain nor any trepidation about the condition, or future condition, of his right hand. The next morning, Dr. and Mrs. Lewis boarded the train for Boston as planned.

Doctor continued to keep the injured hand inside his coat. That same pattern of behavior continued throughout the three-day train trip back to Boston. When Doctor finally arrived home, he looked at the hand; only the slightest trace of a mark remained where the door had slammed on his fingers. There was no discomfort or lameness in his hand. The first day back at his practice, Doctor worked the entire day with no awareness of the injury, but with full awareness of his Guru's intercession.

The Move to California

In the summer of 1945, we did not travel to Los Angeles to be with Master, as we planned instead to leave Boston permanently in October and move to California. The house in Duxbury sold just before we left, and we arrived in Los Angeles on October 31st. During the next four months, we traveled with Master back and forth from Encinitas to Mount Washington. We were always wondering when we were going to be in San Diego as promised. Our goods were stored in a bungalow by the San Diego Church, and I would often ask Master, "When are you going to let us fix up that bungalow?"

In the spring of 1946, however, Master told Doctor that he did not want us to stay in San Diego. We stayed in the northeast room of the Hermitage for the next three years— right next to dear Sister Gyanamata.

In general, this was a very trying period for Doctor. When Doctor gave up his practice, and the Lewis Building was sold, where his office had been for 31 years, he did not say he would continue dentistry, only that he was taking a year's leave of absence. The letters came almost daily, "When will you return? When are you opening your new office?" Finally, Doctor and Master talked the situation over very seriously. Master said, "No more dentistry." And from that point on, Doctor was a much happier person.

Doctor was able to assist in many ways in the projects in which Master was involved. I also seemed to be kept very busy. Many projects were not yet completed; and so the work at this time was truly pioneering.

The Arizona Flagstone Sidewalk

Master was enthusiastic about the Golden World Colony in 1946. One day he called and said that he would like a sidewalk built from the small tower on K Street to the SRF Hotel. We were instructed to build the sidewalk using Arizona flagstone, and I was to choose the largest and reddest pieces. Reverend Michael and some of the boys helped with the project.*

First, the frames were made and the area prepared for cement. Master was pleased with the selection of stones. After much discussion, it was decided that the area around the flagstones would be filled in with green cement. Then the real work began!

Master instructed me to follow the one who put the cement in the frame; I was to see that not one drop of cement was left on the flagstones. A certain portion would be done, and then I would have to start scrubbing the stones. I crawled back and forth for days at a time, cleaning the stones and perfecting the joints. When the sidewalk was finally completed, there was not a single spot of cement on the flagstones.

What vision our Master had! All this was done before any of the Tower was built. The flagstones were laid around the front of the Cafe. Later, after the Cafe was ready for business, the sidewalk around the edge of the Cafe was completed.

---

*Reverend Michael later took the monastic name of Brother Bhaktananda.

Working in the Greenhouse

After the sidewalk project came a five year stay at Paxton's Conservatory. At first, two young men were in charge of the Conservatories. When Master learned that these young men spent a great deal of time sleeping on the benches, he was dreadfully disturbed about the whole situation.

Through a member of the colony, we met a greenhouse grower of many years, a Mr. Miller. Many evenings were spent talking with Mr. Miller; I must say he was a great help to us. At this point, papaya trees filled the greenhouses. Master was eager to expand; so, shortly after our starting in May of 1946, a greenhouse was built between two existing buildings.

At this time, there were a goodly number of young men about, but some were of a strange temperament. The first day the young men were put to work clearing the land between the houses. When I requested one of the young men to do something, at first he just looked at me. Then he threw at me the pitchfork which he had in his hands! Needless to say his stay at the Colony was short-lived. He left that night!

The papaya growing done under Mr. Paxton was a success, but not a money maker. When SRF took over, what was known was learned from Mrs. Paxton (as Mr. Paxton had died) and from a few books. As we learned, papaya is a temperamental fruit, and at the Conservatory, it was grown under glass. Its enemy is the mealy bug, and papaya is not able to tolerate any spray which has an oil base. The best suggestion we received about keeping the trees clean involved eliminating ants. Almost an impossibility! Well, we kept at it for almost two years.

Mr. Miller suggested we should grow potted plants for the market: poinsettias, hydrangeas, violets, tuberous begonias, and then the bumper project, cyclamen. We planted 125,000 seeds, and I believe every seed germinated!

Numerous people helped with raising these plants. Reverend Michael took them to market, and as previous to this Reverend Michael had taken poinsettias to florist shops, he was pretty good in this business.

The greenhouses were heated by a steam boiler, which burned diesel oil. When the green house was purchased, the oil was one and one-half to two cents per gallon; however, in 1951, it was eight cents a gallon. This made operating the greenhouse a very expensive proposition, so eventually it was sold through the efforts of Rajarsi, Doctor, and a few others.

Work at the Greenhouse was extremely difficult. The hours were very long, and the equipment was obsolete; but nevertheless, I learned many valuable lessons during this five year period. I pray I never have to suffer again the pangs of owning or working in a greenhouse! When Master first put me in the greenhouse, I said I would give it five years. And as it just happened to turn out, it was exactly five years when Doctor and I left.

After leaving the greenhouse, Doctor was able to do so much more in terms of helping people with their spiritual life. My new work seemed to be centered completely on the maintenance and upkeep of the Hermitage. There was also some work with the gardens and food for the restaurant. This I enjoyed.

Doctor's Hat

Twenty-Nine Palms, in the late forties, was a quiet desert community, far different from today with the nearby military installations and all the activity they bring.* In the forties, vast stretches of desert could be seen, unfettered by human life. The Joshua trees were everywhere. In the late afternoon, nature and elements joined forces to highlight

---

*The following story was told to Brenda Lewis, by her mother, Mildred Lewis.

the terrain. It was in this setting that Master had a little desert retreat house.

In the desert beauty, Master and Doctor walked together, ruminating on the "Master Painter" that the Guru had written about; surely, there was no greater evidence of His artistic hand than this. Doctor was always dressed—even in the desert—as it was part of his New England heritage. He was wearing a kind of fedora, which his daughter had given him. She felt that the blue hue of the hat matched his eyes. Because Brenda had given it to him, and because he just plain liked it, he was dismayed when a gust of wind blew it off his head, causing it to tumble with the fast wind out across the desert.

Master and Doctor both ran after the elusive chapeau, but the wind was too fast for them, and darkness, which sometimes falls quickly in the desert, was soon upon them. They walked back to where Mrs. Lewis was waiting in the car and drove back to the little retreat house. Upon their return Master assured Doctor that if he went back in the morning to the spot where the hat had disappeared, he would find it.

With first light illuminating the desert, Doctor began the drive back to the place where they had parked the previous afternoon. But the desert looked far different in the morning, and he wasn't certain of the spot—the wind had erased the tire tracks. His intuition must have been razor sharp, for he stopped the car where he at last felt they had been the night before, got out, and started hiking. After tracking through the desert sands until the sun was high in the sky, he looked ahead, and, lo and behold, there was the blue hat, half-hidden in a creosote bush. Doctor smiled. He walked to the spot, donned the hat with a gleeful pat, and walked back toward the car. His mind soared upon Master's words in the *Autobiography of a Yogi:* "for whenever the joy of meditation has returned subconsciously during my active hours, I have been subtly directed to adopt the right course in everything, even *details*." Doctor drove contentedly back toward the retreat house. He would tell Master that his, Master's, instructions found fruition in the morning air of the desert.

Watermelon Story

In the late 1940's, when Doctor and Mrs. Lewis were living in Encinitas, they often went on rides with Master and some of the disciples.* One of Master's favorite rides was to the country area east of Encinitas, where they sometimes took picnic lunches and enjoyed the beautiful scenery. Master had many friends who had ranches in this area, where he would go searching for delicious fruits, vegetables and litchi nuts.†

On one such trip someone gave Master a huge watermelon, and he was extremely pleased to receive this gift. On the way home Mrs. Lewis at first wondered, "What is he going to do with that huge melon?" Through her intuition, it then dawned on her!

Arriving in Encinitas quite late, Master announced, as was his custom, that everyone should go to the front lawn for exercises. After the exercises, some of those present were heading slowly towards their quarters in the Hermitage, when Master announced that everyone should come to the kitchen. He told them, "We are going to make watermelon [rind] pickle." Anyone who has made this pickle knows it involves a long process of cutting the watermelon in exact-sized pieces, preparing the syrup, cooking it, and repeating three times the process with the syrup.

All of the cooking utensils were made ready, and the melon was scrubbed, then peeled. Master was directing the project at this time. Then, after some time had passed,

---

*The following story was told to Brenda Lewis by her mother, Mildred Lewis.

†Litchi nuts come from the litchi tree and are eaten dried or preserved. Master used to serve these in a syrup over ice cream.

Mrs. Lewis noticed that some of the disciples had left the kitchen quietly; and finally, only Master and Mrs. Lewis were working. And then Master said, "I'm leaving now, you stay here and finish the job." She continued her task for a few minutes; then she walked down the hall to her room. She was very upset and confronted Dr. Lewis, saying, "I am not going to stay up all night and do that job all alone. Everyone has left the kitchen." Dr. Lewis said, "I think you had better go back and complete the job as Master told you to do it."

The result was that Mrs. Lewis did stay up all night and complete the job. She never experienced fatigue again!

Remembering Sister Gyanamata

In the latter months of Sister's life, she especially liked to hear Doctor play the chants for the Thursday evening class. It was arranged that Sister's door in the Hermitage be left open, so the lady who attended her during the night could attend the lecture given by Dr. Lewis. It was my job to sit in the hallway, so that I could answer the telephone or Sister's call bell. This routine was followed for many, many Thursday nights. Rarely was I called by Sister; however, on one particular Thursday night, she called me. I went immediately to her room, where she asked that I arrange the shawl over her shoulders. Then she requested me to draw up a chair close to her bedside.

"Mrs. Lewis," she said, "there is something I want to tell you tonight." I said, "Yes, Sister, what is it?" She said, I want you to know that ever since I have known you and Doctor, all these years, you have never done anything to displease me." How sweet those words were coming from this beautiful Soul! The following day Doctor and I left for our vacation. That was the last talk I had with Sister; she passed away the following week on November 17, 1951.

Doctor's Unceasing Dedication

After Master passed away, Doctor became very involved in giving classes for the monks, just as Master had wanted. Every week I would drive Doctor to Mount Washington, so he could give the classes. During this time I would visit with Ma Durga and then drive Doctor back to Encinitas. It was not long before the monks in Hollywood and Lake Shrine complained that they were not able to attend the classes being given at Mount Washington. As a result, the classes were held Friday nights in India Hall, Hollywood.

Before long, a group of young men active in the church wanted to join the monks for their meditation. There was a class on the theory and then a long meditation. Then it was thought best to exclude the public at the men's meditation, so a separate meditation was held for the lay people (men only). Not long after this, there was a cry from the women—they, too, wanted to attend the meditation. This is how the very active meditation group on Friday nights, which is still being held, was started.

Doctor served the Fellowship one hundred percent, as he did in everything he ever undertook. No matter how trying the circumstances, we kept on faithfully working for Master. Doctor never had a Sunday off: he went to Los Angeles every Friday, leaving Encinitas at 2 P.M. and not arriving home until 2 A.M. or later. This procedure went on until two weeks before his passing on April 13, 1960. It was a marvel to all how he kept going, but I am sure God and Guru were with him all the way. During these years, our daughter Brenda served him as secretary and driver.

The Borrego Retreat

One day Madame Amelita Galli Curci* telephoned Doctor at the Hermitage. She asked whether he would be trav-

---

*Mrs. Homer Samuels was her married name; Madame Amelita Galli-Curci was a noted opera singer.

eling to Borrego within the next few days; Doctor told her that he planned to go the following day, Saturday.

[Doctor was going to see Rajarsi, who had a farm in Borrego—a desert town some 100 miles northeast of Encinitas; Madame Galli-Curci also had a home in Borrego, as the following story describes. — The Editor]

Two weeks previously Madame Galli-Curci had had to leave the house in Borrego on short notice, as her husband had experienced a very severe attack of emphysema. Madame Galli-Curci was uneasy about how she had left things—and whether she had turned off the electricity and the water—and so she wanted Doctor to check these utilities for her. At the close of her conversation with Doctor, she said, "Lewis, why don't you buy the house? Homer can never go to the desert again."

At noon on Saturday, we left for Borrego to carry vegetables to Rajarsi from the Encinitas gardens and also to complete Madame Galli-Curci's request. On reaching Borrego, Doctor and I went to see Rajarsi. Doctor told Rajarsi about his conversation with Madame Galli-Curci. And then Doctor asked Rajarsi if he would object to our having a house in Borrego. His answer was, "Of course not. If you don't buy it, I will."

We then went to Wagon Road and found the house. Doctor opened the door and went in. I followed and, as I stepped in, I said, "If I had the money, I would buy this house." Sitting in a chair which he always later used, Doctor replied with an old English quip: "I knew my goose was cooked."

We then left Borrego, returning via Rancho Santa Fe to deliver the message that all was well at the house. Immediately Homer asked Doctor, "Why don't you buy it, Doctor? I will sell it to you completely furnished." Doctor informed him that we would buy it. During this time, I remained in the car, thinking that possibly Homer was worse and that Doctor was sitting with him, as he often did, in meditation.

As Doctor headed back to Encinitas, he told me we had purchased the house. Later the Samuels kindly told us, "We didn't build the house for us; we built it for the Lewises, and how the Lewises have enjoyed the house. Hope it will be enjoyed by Master's devotees for years to come."

The idea of a house started before Master passed away in 1952. Doctor often said that he would like to get a little place in the desert, where the atmosphere is dry. Well, it did come!

Each week we would go to Borrego, leaving either late on Monday evening or early Tuesday morning. We would stay until Thursday afternoon and return in time for Doctor to give the Thursday evening lecture, which took place in the Hermitage. Summer and winter, this program went on. Doctor would have Wednesday as his long meditation day; Wednesday evening and Thursday, he would prepare for the Sunday sermon he gave at the San Diego Church. Once a month, he also gave a Hollywood Sunday service and an evening meditation service at Lake Shrine.

No changes were made in the house on Wagon Road until after Doctor passed away, and then not for four years. I had an urge to build a chapel, but at this time, one of my friends who was visiting in Borrego suggested that first I enlarge the original house or add a small guest house.

It was a big decision for me to take a loan out. My Borrego visitor graciously carried the loan for some time, then I carried if for about five years, when through God's grace I received a gift that completely paid the loan off. That was a great relief!

The Smallest Desire

During a world tour in 1962, Mrs. Lewis and Aunt Dolly, the sister of Dr. Lewis, visited Madame Helene Tissot in Switzerland.* During their visit, Madame Tissot arranged

---

*Madame Tissot was a devoted disciple of Paramahansa Yogananda who made a great effort to establish SRF Centers in Switzerland. This story was

a trip to Zurich for Mrs. Lewis and Aunt Dolly. This allowed Madame Tissot an opportunity to visit a sick friend, and at the same time, it also allowed Mrs. Lewis and Aunt Dolly to spend some time with Madame Redard at her antique shop.*

In due course, Mrs. Lewis and Aunt Dolly arrived at the antique shop. While waiting for Madame Redard to finish a transaction with a customer, Aunt Dolly and Mrs. Lewis browsed through the intriguing shop. Aunt Dolly quietly said to Mrs. Lewis (well away from Madame Redard's hearing), "If you could have anything you wanted in this shop, what would you choose?" Mrs. Lewis selected a very tiny old brass iron used for ironing tiny clothes for children. Then she asked Aunt Dolly what she would like. Aunt Dolly looked around the displays and pointed to a very small pewter pitcher way up high on a shelf. She thought because it was very small, it could be tucked into her suitcase easily, and at the same time, it would be a reminder of this visit to Switzerland.

After a while Madame Redard finished with her customer and rejoined the two ladies, asking if they would like something in particular as souvenirs from Zurich. Mother said to Madame Redard, "Why don't you select something for us?" Madame Redard got up from her chair and walked straight to the shelf where the tiny iron was displayed, picked up the iron, and handed it to Mrs. Lewis. Then she reached up to the high shelf and handed Aunt Dolly the pewter pitcher. God fulfills the smallest desires of true devotees!

The Borrego Retreat[†] Evolves

In all the projects I have had, and I always do have, a tremendous feeling of guidance. I realize now the reason

---
written by Brenda Lewis. — The Editor

*Madame Redard was a devoted member of SRF in Switzerland.

[†]Mrs. Lewis was fond of calling the Borrego Retreat *Ananda Lok*, the place of Bliss.

Master always kept pushing to complete a building which was solely done for God and Guru. The purpose has to be right in order to venture into making it a more useful and available spot for peace and quiet, away from the worldly activity which drains one's energy.

Having completed the building of a small guest house, I was still not satisfied. I had not yet built a chapel. While I was carrying the loan on the guest house, I became determined not to add any more loans to my life. After giving this chapel idea great thought, and after asking God and Master to guide my decisions, in January of 1968, I made an appointment in Borrego with the architect who designed the house.

When he arrived the appointed morning, I told him of my great desire to build a chapel. Some years previously, the architect had read *The Autobiography Of A Yogi*. He said he knew that I would want to inculcate some of the ideas or trends of Hinduism or East Indian culture into the design of the chapel, and so he would read the book once again. Our two hour meeting seemed to fire me even more to build this chapel, and I wanted to tell Sister Durga Mata about it. At that time, during the winter and spring months, she was spending quite a bit of time in Borrego.

When I next saw Durga Ma, I greeted her, saying, "I have something to tell you." I told her about the meeting with the architect and the plans to build a chapel in the desert in memory of Doctor. She was extremely enthusiastic about the idea. Leaving the room for a moment, she soon returned. Pressing a twenty dollar bill in my hand, she said, "Let this start the fund. I know it will grow." How true were her words!

From that day on until its completion in October of 1969, all monies came forth through the Grace of God and Master. I never asked for one cent. To me this was a miracle, for I did not have the money to spend. But I did know that there was going to be a chapel in honor of Doctor who loved the desert, but most of all, Doctor had such beautiful spiritual growth at this spot.

The pictures of the Masters on the altar, an outstanding bit of work, were done by a German photographer in San Diego. This photographer also did the enlargement of the picture of Doctor seated on the stage of the San Diego Church. Beside the altar is a picture of Master done in pastels around which hangs Master's silk scarf.

One day a dear friend of ours paid a visit and was most enthusiastic upon seeing the chapel. As he was leaving he turned to me and said, "I want to send you a gift when I get back to the city." The gift came as promised; and as it turned out, it was the right amount needed for the air conditioner! Scenarios like this were replayed time and again in improving the Borrego Retreat.

The Chapel was dedicated on November 1, 1969; we invited sixty people, and fifty-eight were present. Sister Daya Mata was in India at this time, and so for the dedication, Brother Anandamoy and a few monks drove from Los Angeles. Brenda played the harmonium for the chanting. After a period of meditation, Brother Anandamoy gave a talk. Mrs. Lewis then thanked those who had worked on the project for their respect and cooperation.

It was a beautiful day, this All Saints Day, in Borrego. It was a little warmer than usual, but still very clear, and not windy. In the patio, tables were set for the guests, who were served a buffet luncheon.

Over the years, many, many people have visited the chapel. Those who come look forward to their meditations. Each time I enter, I feel that Master and Doctor are smiling, and Master is (playfully) saying, "Remember how she was in the beginning?" It is all your work, Master.

Throughout the years, a number of other additions were also made. So many friends and visitors touchingly contributed from their hearts. They and the Great Ones know who they are; all comes through the grace of God and Master.

Only a few of these I'll mention here: the lot next to the chapel was acquired; Sister Durga encouraged me to make a number of changes in the original house; a fireplace was added; the kitchen remodeled; and, during 1976–1977, a beautiful Annex Guest House was added. As one enters the annex, there is a beautiful picture of Master, a copy of a painting by Master's brother Sananda Lal Ghosh. Always I feel that Master would love the Borrego Retreat. He enjoys it through all of his devotees who use it.

We have established a very good routine at Borrego. The Chapel is open very early in the morning. Anyone staying at the retreat may use it as they wish. Evening meditation usually begins at 8:30 P.M., which starts with a period of chanting.

Over the years, I made a decision that I would improve the property and take care of it to the best of my ability, with the help of Master and God's guidance. All efforts are made to keep the property in good condition, as Master would want; the grounds are kept beautifully by a man who lives in Borrego.

Living in San Diego all these years has also been very rewarding. At times it has been difficult; but, nevertheless, I am blessed to be on Master's property [at the San Diego Church] through his foresight. As the Master would say often to Doctor and me, it was filmed and finished.

Photos From 1920-1921

Swami Yogananda

Mildred

Doctor

Bren

Brad

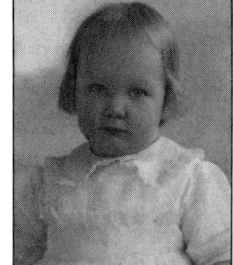

24 Electric Ave

Doctor Lewis, 1948

Chapter 2

Doctor Lewis Reminisces

These stories that I am about to tell had a beginning late one October afternoon, as I was leaving my office in Davis Square, Somerville, Massachusetts.* Walking diagonally across that square, a strange figure passed me; a fast-moving figure, clothed in an orange coat, puttees, yellow shoes, and with a large orange turban on his head. Of course, in the surprise of seeing such a figure on the streets of Somerville, I turned as he passed and watched as he disappeared across the square. Little did I realize the part that this strange-looking man was to play in my life, for it was none other than the Master, at that time known as Swami Yogananda, later known as Paramahansa Yogananda.

Although I did not meet the Master until Christmas Eve of the same year, Mrs. Lewis shook hands with him, about a month later from the time I saw him in Davis Square, at a metaphysical meeting at which he was the guest speaker. She told me about meeting this strange person from India, and we discussed the pros and cons, but there the subject dropped.

A few days before Christmas Eve, a friend of mine, Mrs. Ward Hasey, who later received the title of Sister Yogamata from the Master, called me on the telephone and asked me, or suggested strongly, that I make an appointment to meet

---
*Doctor Lewis taped these stories in 1958.

Swami Yogananda, who was staying in Boston at that time. I was not too much impressed, but she insisted; and, as she and I had been together working in different metaphysical organizations, I at last agreed to call him on the phone and to make an appointment. This I did, and on Christmas Eve, I kept my first appointment with the Master in Unity House, Park Square, Boston, Massachusetts. I had not been enthusiastic about meeting him, for the simple reason that I was somewhat prejudiced; also, I had heard many stories about the fakirs of India and their strange customs and doings, and I personally did not want to be fooled or to be taken in, so to speak, by such people; however, as I have said, I did condescend to meet the Master at this time.

And I well remember, as I first came into the room, he looked at me with a little smile; and of course, I looked at him with the same kind of a smile—as much as to say that I was here, but I did not want to be taken advantage of. We exchanged a few greetings, sat down, and began to discuss various questions along religious lines.

Finally, I said to him, "Sir, I have searched in many places—in scriptures, and I have asked many people about such passages as 'If thine eye be single, thy whole body shall be full of light'* and other similar questions of a metaphysical nature." And I said, "I have been unable to receive any answer; no one has been able to give me a satisfactory answer or show me any such light." And the Master said to me at that time, quoting Jesus' words, "Can the blind lead the blind? They both fall into the ditch."† These words impressed me, because they were from our Bible, and it was a reasonable answer given to my question. Being an American, I, of course, said right off, "Have you seen such things? Do you know the single eye?" I remember Master said, "I think so." And I said, "Do you think I could see such things?" And he said, "I think so." Of course, I said,

---
*Matthew 6:22.
†Luke 6:39.

"Well, show me." And so he smiled and said, "All right, in a little while." And so we talked on further in the same vein.

Then he procured a tiger skin and laid it on the floor. He sat down on one end, at the head, and he said to me, "Would you mind sitting down in front of me?" He was sitting cross-legged; and of course, I had never to my knowledge ever sat cross-legged under such circumstances. But I said, "Yes, certainly," and somehow I got down cross-legged. But I can assure you it was not the lotus posture!

And so as we sat there in close proximity, the Master looked at me straight in the eye, and he said, "Doctor, will you always love me as I love you?" Well, I had never been talked to in such a manner before, but I looked at him, and I saw something that I had not seen before in anyone, and so I quickly said, "Yes, I will." With that, I remember distinctly the Master rubbed his hands together, and he said, "That's fine. I take charge of your life." Well, just what that meant at the time I didn't know, but at least I felt it was all right, so I acquiesced, and then we proceeded.

As I sat in front of him and he calmed my restless mind, he placed his forehead against my forehead. He told me to lift my eyes and to look at the point between the eyebrows, which I did. There appeared the great spiritual light of the spiritual eye.

The Master did not suggest anything that I see; he did not in any way influence me through suggestion, but what I saw came in a natural way. I was fully conscious, fully awake, fully alert, and I saw the spiritual eye, because the Master stilled the waves of my mind and allowed my own intuition of the soul to show me the door—the spiritual eye—the reflected light of the medulla center. As I looked further in the great golden light, the spiritual eye came, with its dark center manifesting the Christ Consciousness within me, and finally the little silver star in the center, the epitome of Cosmic Consciousness.

Of course, I was naturally overwhelmed at having found someone who could show me the inner reality that is within each one of us. I had meditated as best I could, following various techniques. I perceived the light around my head on the right and on the left, but I could not focus it, as it was vague. But when the Master focused my mind and showed me where to look, and made it possible for me to see the spiritual eye, then I realized that he was not an ordinary person, but a man far different from the ordinary run of men who profess to know about such spiritual things.

We talked for a few minutes. And then once more he pressed his forehead against my forehead; it was then that I saw the great light of the thousand-rayed lotus—the most exquisite thing that can be seen, with its many, many rays of silver leaves. At the bottom of the thousand-rayed lotus, I could see outlined in the denser light the walls of the large arteries at the base of the brain. And lo and behold! As I watched, little sparks of light inside the arteries were bobbing along, striking the wall of the artery, as they passed before my vision. These were the blood corpuscles, each with its little spark of astral light manifesting as it carried out its duty in God's play of light.

Of course, seeing these wonderful things, I was most grateful for having met such a man of realization. And I remember what the Master said. He said, "If you will allow me to discipline you, and if you follow regularly the path I lay down, these things will be with you always." I have endeavored to do that; and I can testify that the words of the Master came true.

One thing he did ask me, though. He said, "Promise me one thing: that you will not avoid me." Of course, I was only too glad to promise that, after seeing the wonderful things that I did and [after] having the realization [I did.] Little did I realize how difficult it would be not to avoid him in the difficult middle ground of discipline. But I kept my promise and did not avoid him; and thus I was able to be saved from much suffering and much delusion.

When our spiritual feast was over, the time had slipped away; it was in the early hours of Christmas Day when I left the Master. It had been my custom always to be at home Christmas Eve to decorate the tree and to be with Mrs. Lewis and the children; but in this case, somehow, those things were secondary compared to the spiritual food that I attained on that Christmas Eve.

And so when I did come home, having expected to be only perhaps an hour or two with the Master, Mrs. Lewis was waiting for me with the famous rolling pin, but all the way home, the great spiritual light was before me. And when I came into the house and met her, I remember decidedly how cross she was. And she had reason to be so; but seeing my face, evidently the effect of the spiritual baptism which the Master gave me—seeing that, she was unable to cause me any distress.

I remember it took about a month of careful intrigue under the Master's direction to bring about a meeting between them, which was done in the house of Sister Yogamata. After that meeting, which only required a few moments, a wonderful relationship between them was re-established; her loyalty and devotion have not wavered ever since.

A Five-Hour Meditation at Plum Island

In the Spring of 1921, around April, we all decided that we would take a few days and travel up to the North Shore, as it is called, of Massachusetts, to the summer home of Sister Yogamata, and there spend a few days. Those of you who know New England realize that in April the North Shore is very cold and very disagreeable; but we went there, and although it was a summer house, we thought we could keep warm and build fires. So off we started. We arrived there, and as evening came, the fires were lit.

I remember the Master said, as he saw us rubbing our hands together and saying, "Oooh, Oooh, Oooh," and he wondered just what that was. But he said, "I found out all right later that night." When we went to bed, he had lots of blankets; he got in with clothes, shoes and all. During the night in the intense cold and dampness, he pulled the blankets up to his head and neck. It was quite a sight in the morning to see his feet sticking out below the blankets. I remember that he said then, "Now I realize what you meant by going, 'Oooh, Oooh, Oooh.'"

The next day was a clear, sunny day, but as I have said, at that time of year, it is still cold and penetrating. There is a nice breakwater which runs out from the beach in front of the cottage in which we stayed. As we were walking up and down the beach—the Master and I discussing spiritual things and talking about God—he suddenly spied this breakwater made of huge granite blocks. And he said, "Let us meditate, Doctor. This is a wonderful place by the ocean."

So we went out on the breakwater and sat down and started to meditate. The tide was out and we were safely perched up on the rocks. That was my first experience of any kind of meditation, especially under those conditions. Well, the first hour, I don't believe there were any rocks any harder than those rocks, but somehow I hung on, saying, "If the Master can sit here, I can sit here—even if it kills me." So, as I have said, after about an hour, my body became numb, and by the Grace of God and the Master's help, I was able to stay there.

And do you know that we stayed there for five hours? Suddenly I was aroused by the Master saying, "Doctor, Doctor, Doctor, let's go, let's get out of here." The waves were coming up, breaking around those big stones, and so we got out from that precarious position. Although it was quite an ordeal, it was a great blessing. Because of that great effort I made, thereafter, meditation was not a hardship, but my efforts were made much easier by the endurance of that discipline. And so I will always remember the five hours on

Master Takes Care of Doctor's Family

that breakwater at Plum Island, Massachusetts.

A short time after the Master's arrival in Boston, he began to give Sunday lectures in a little hall near Copley Square, known as Faelton Hall. After the Sunday lectures, I would go to his room, where he would cook little dishes for me. We would discuss God and the Great Ones and such things, and then usually he would come out to the house and stay during the week, until his lecture on Thursday night—his Thursday night class. During those times, many nights were spent in discussion and in listening to the stories of his life, which came out later in his *Autobiography*.

I remember that one Sunday evening I had gone to his room. He was preparing food when the telephone rang, and I answered it. Mrs. Lewis had called me to tell me that my little daughter had just had another convulsion. I had schooled her in the necessary things to do in those cases, but she called me, and the Master sensed something was wrong. I remember he said, "What is it, Doctor, what is it?" Well, after talking with Mrs. Lewis, I hung up the phone and told him that my daughter had had another convulsion.

I remember how his faced changed. He stepped behind a little screen which separated the "kitchen" from the rest of his room. It was only a few moments before he came out, his faced bathed in smiles, and he said, "Don't worry, Doctor, she'll be all right, and she will never have another." I remember that night, after we finished our meal and talked a little bit, we went to my home. The Master sat by my daughter's crib all night. And of course, she has never had anything like that happen since. And so it is those things—and many other things which I will tell you—which make us realize how blessed we were to have the Master present with us in our own home.

A Time of Great Blessings

As I have said, many nights were spent in listening to his wonderful words and his experiences and romping about the house as brothers keeping Mrs. Lewis in a state of turmoil—which seemed to be just what we wanted; but in spite of all of those things, that wonderful reverence and devotion was never tainted in the least bit; and the Master was our Master in spite of the close relationship. I remember one occasion that I slept with the Master. He asked me to sleep with him. Well, I thought that was all right. Later I remember he told me that was one of the greatest honors that a disciple can have to sleep with his Master.*

And so days passed; then the hot weather began to come. Many hours on the hot days were spent discussing God and the Great Ones. I remember sipping the wonderful limeade which the Master made, which he alone could make in just the right way. And those days of being with him, enjoying great quantities of his limeade, certainly will never be forgotten.

The Master Helps Doctor and His Family

In telling you this story about the Master, I do not want to give you the impression that he and his spiritual powers were used to collect bad debts; but, nevertheless, this is the way it happened.

Shortly before I met the Master, just a few months before, I became acquainted with a gentleman. And through

---

*This privilege was also given to the young Yogananda by his Guru, Swami Sri Yukteswarji of Puri. The significance of sleeping with a Guru is that the tremendous high vibration of a man who is one with God is absorbed (according to the power of the disciples receptivity) in sleep, thereby destroying mountains of karma and uplifting the disciple, so that every cell of his body is electrified by the power of God flowing through the liberated Master. Great spiritual, mental, and physical healings have occurred when such blessings are received. — The Editor him I had some business dealings in stocks and so forth. Although he did not cheat me deliberately, perhaps he did use the fact that I had taken him into the family and he had gotten into my good graces: he used that to sell me certain securities that were not of the highest type.

So after a while, the friendship terminated, and he still owed me some money. Just about then the Master came along. In discussing certain things, his being new in this country, from a foreign land, I said to him one time, "How do I know that you are not like a certain gentleman who came not long ago? I befriended him, and he took advantage of that friendship. How do I know that perhaps you may not be in the same category?"

"Well," he said, "of course, we have to be careful of those things, but with a truly religious man, that is not possible." And then I told him about this gentleman and of the activities that went on between us; and he said, "Well, I will tell you that he was not good for you." Then he told me out of a clear sky, he said—and he named the gentleman: call him "Mr. Black"—"Mr. Black is now in Lowell, Massachusetts. If you send Mildred up there, she will be able to get the money he owes you." I did send Mrs. Lewis up that day, and she found the gentleman at the given address. She returned with the money. And of course, even when things are taken in the light of Divine Consciousness, even such things are taken care of, through God's wonderful protection through the Guru.

Doctor Nearly Gets Wet

The next incident that I want to relate to you is perhaps one of the most astonishing happenings in my relationship with the Master. I certainly believe that it was through his intervention that I am here at this time telling these stories.

It happened on a hot Sunday afternoon in July, 1921. We had gone to my father's summer place on Plymouth Bay in Duxbury, Massachusetts. There we had gone in a small boat, the three of us—my father, my brother and myself. We were about two miles off shore when it was quite evident that a very severe squall was about to break. The sky had a very foreboding look, and huge thunderheads had arisen in the northwest. Then the darkness began to settle in that region. The wind had died down. Seeing our predicament, we started to row back toward the shore.

The boat was not too large a boat, so that two (one with each oar) could make some headway. And so we rowed like mad in the direction of home. We were unable to reach the shore, being about a half mile off shore, when the terrific squall broke. Luckily, we had a huge anchor, which was thrown overboard with a great rope; but in spite of that, unless there had been some intervention, I know we would not have survived such wind, rain, hail, thunder and lightening.

I remember, as I peaked out from under the canvas which we were holding over the cockpit, that I wondered just what it would be like when the end came. Then I remembered: the family, the children came to my consciousness, and the thought of leaving them. And then came the thought of the Master. We had just started on such a wonderful spiritual relationship, and now that had to end.

I remember what a decided pang came into my heart as those things came to my consciousness. And then I remembered the words of the Master, which he had said not too long before that. He said, "Remember Doctor, when you are in the Om vibration, when your consciousness is centered in the Christ Center in the forehead, when you merge in that Om vibration, nothing can harm you." And so I lifted my eyes and looked there where he had told me. And behold a great light, a great light in the shape of a large spiritual eye came right in the midst of that storm. And with it, there descended upon me such a consciousness of peace and security, that I knew nothing could touch me.

In due time the storm broke, and a large motorboat put

out to rescue us and to tow us to shore. There was great rejoicing. The whole colony had gathered together on the shore during the storm, fearing that we would be lost. And there was great rejoicing and reunion.

The rest of the day was spent at my father's home. Late that night, I arrived back in my own home in Somerville, Massachusetts. Just as I entered the door, the telephone rang. I answered, and the Master's voice said to me, "Well, Doctor, you came near getting wet today, didn't you?" Of course, I didn't grasp or realize at first what he meant, until the second time he said it. Then I realized that he must have known something of what had happened. He was, by the way, the first to know, but he never said another word about it.

It was not until several years later, when I happened to be talking with Sister Yogamata—who, by the way, was the first Sister created in America in Boston—and she told me that at that precise time, about 3:15 on that Sunday afternoon several years before, that the Master and she were seated in her parlor. He was reading Emerson's essay, "On the Sea," when, she said, suddenly he threw down the book, jumped to his feet, and began pacing the floor saying, "Sister, the Doctor is in trouble, serious trouble; serious trouble, I tell you."

Well, when I found out that, at the first opportunity I preceded to pin the Master down, so to speak; and I at last gained an admission that he had seen just what was happening. This story shows that a true master, like Paramahansa Yogananda, is without doubt One with God's Omniscience. And as His Omniscience knows all things, He sees all things. One who is One with that Omniscience can likewise be cognizant of all things that are happening.*

---

*Shortly after Master's passing Doctor was conducting a class for the monks. He told them that if they had known what Master was, they would have fallen procumbent at his feet.

The Master Rescues Doctor's Health

After a stay of three years in Boston, Master started on his trip to spread Self-Realization, first in New York, and then in other places. In January of the same year in which he left for New York, I remember, I was discussing with him my spiritual progress. As was my custom, I always asked him how I was getting along, and I asked for suggestions. He said, "You are doing all right, but watch you health next summer," and that was all that I could extract from him.

As time went on, I forgot his warnings, being taken up with a busy practice. But when summer came, I soon remembered, because I was taken with a very depressing, serious condition with the body, which caused me great pain and made the practice of my profession very difficult. Somehow I kept going, but this one particular day, when it reached its height, I was at my summer place in Duxbury, the same place about which you heard of in the story of the storm. On this particular Wednesday, I remember, I was suffering quite severely, so much so that our most beautiful dog climbed up on the sofa beside me and lapped my face, as she seemed to be trying to comfort me as best she could.

Somehow I got through the afternoon and went upstairs to bed. In the middle of the night or early morning there was quite a commotion out in the driveway, and I heard someone calling, "Doctor, Doctor, Doctor Lewis." In due time we came downstairs and found that the Master had come up from New York. He had somehow been able to procure an automobile and a driver, and he had one or two people with him. He had come all the way up from New York, and he arrived at the hour of my greatest need, in that early hour of the morning. I remember that after greetings, he came inside. How anxiously I awaited the time when I could tell him just how miserably I was feeling!

He didn't seem to pay much attention, until finally he did take me aside, and we went upstairs and talked about my condition. I told him how really badly I was feeling. He didn't say much, he smiled a little and said, "You'll be all right. You just do what I tell you, and God will take care of you."

I remember he gave me a very peculiar, drastic remedy. It is not possible to tell it at this time, but if I ever find any devotee who needs it, I will without any hesitation give it to him. I started in with the remedy, and my improvement took place right off. I steadily improved, until finally the malady left me and has never returned.

I remember that when the Master wrote me from New York again, he said, "The condition was really serious, and, of course, it needed a very drastic, serious remedy and a unique remedy to take care of the situation." Once more this story shows that to the humble devotee who is really one hundred percent in tune with the Master, the Master never forgets him, for God has ordained that the Guru will stay with the humble devotee, until finally, He takes him home.

A few years later, the Master returned to Boston to visit us, and I was supposed to meet him at the Back Bay Station. I was delayed for just a few minutes by parking; he in the meantime had gone to the telephone and he was trying to call me. Just about that time I entered the waiting room of the station, which was filled with people. Suddenly I heard this voice calling, "Doctor, Doctor, Doctor Lewis," and in just a few moments, I saw the Master coming from the direction of the telephone booth through the crowd to find me. I later found out that he was trying to call when suddenly he saw my face. Not following convention to hang up the telephone, he left it in mid-air and started calling my name as he came out and found me.

Swami Yogananda, 1921

Chapter 3

Letters from Paramahansa Yogananda

The following letters from Paramahansa Yogananda to Doctor and Mildred Lewis span a period of thirty years from 1921–1951. Arranged in chronological order, they are unique in showing the Master over a long period of time, practically covering the entire time the Master spent in the West. Not only do these letters show some of the Guru's wisdom and practical advice, but they also show the personal, warm and affectionate manner he had with his disciples—almost childlike—in inviting them to spend time with him or to exchange Christmas presents. The Master would say, and others would also notice, that after Doctor and Mildred had visited Mount Washington and returned to Boston, that he [Yogananda] would lose his appetite. Such was his affection for them. At other times, the letters show how he could be stern or forceful, as he desired.

Just as some prefer a more polished, edited version in poetry and prose, others prefer to read an author's earliest works. These letters are presented much as they originally appeared: except for an occasional change of punctuation, or a minor orthographic change in words to make their use consistent with common usage, nothing has been added; on the other hand, some matters dealing with health, money, and personal issues have been omitted. For example, some of the Master's specific recommendations for Doctor Lewis' health were meant for him alone, and it would be inappropriate to try to generalize his advice to anyone else.

The sample below shows the Master's handwriting:

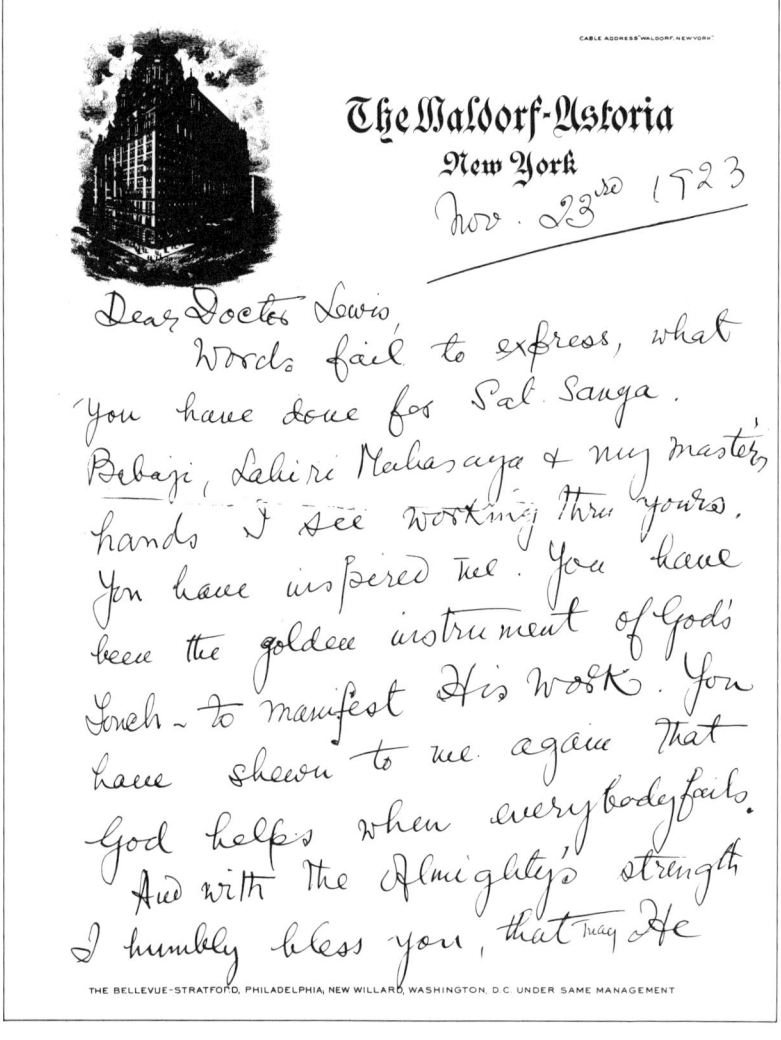

Lester Terrace
West Somerville, Mass.
Friday, August 12, 1921

Dear Mildred,*

Glad to receive your letter today. I wonder why your letter dated Tuesday arrived here today. During the daytime mostly I am here but in the night I generally live in Cambridge.

I am glad you praise the "turnip creole" but do not forget to sing the message of Sat-Sanga along with that. The Sat-Sanga is the salt of the soup without that it is tasteless. So I shall always be still more glad, if I find you all fostering and spreading broadcast of the seeds of Sat-Sanga. Don't underestimate the soul's power within you—do at least something which you can.

However, now to turnip soup. You know the peeling and cutting them into chips along with potatoes and summer squash. Smear them with saffron or a lot of red paprika and salt. Fry them very well. Then pour water sufficiently to boil them. Add plenty of sugar and huge quantity of butter. (Cover the soup when boiling) and then when the water becomes thick and all things are well cooked take it down (No Garam Mashala). Eat it hot.

You can give the Lewises a taste of my onion rings—cut onions in round rings—dip them in beaten egg with salt and paprika (and Garam Mashala if possible) and then fry in deep fat. ...

At the same time don't think I am discouraging you in any way in giving people the enjoyment of a soup. What I say is you should not stop there—you should always lie in readiness to give something more along with that whenever they are unawares and sober. My blessings to you, Doctor,

---
*First letter received by Mildred Lewis from S. Y.

Mr. Baba and Miss Lewis. Greetings to Dolly and her sister.

With Best Wishes,

Swami Yogananda Giri

Sat-Sanga Hermitage
North Waltham, Mass.
August 4, 1922

Dear Doctor,

Mighty pleased to receive your letter. Yes, you are the same as ever—you reveal it in your writing. I am glad of it and shall be delighted still more if you remain the same as ever and with the progress of days make more improvement on that.

It is elegant to know that you are enjoying the long-hoped for rest after a year's hard toil. Well, the outlook of your affairs will improve just as you have added to your flesh and spirit. Real rest you know by this time is in meditation—other times the mind is constantly tossing identified with the motions of ever-changing thoughts. Unceasing, untiring patience, adamant will, unflagging zeal—wins the victor's laurel for the right devotee. Do not fail to improve your better half by good and kind advices—suggestions thrown in during the gaps of rest of the mind or pleasantness—entering into the receiver's inner being and becoming part and parcel of her. This requires patience and watchfulness—the teacher has to wait for such suitable moments. Forced suggestions hurled at others in impatience are repelled back quickly by them. By quick work we sometimes lose time, in the hope of saving it.

How is little Brenda and Bradford—remember me to them and Mildred. My blessing to you all. Please don't be hen-pecked in echoing the "Mosquito Stuff."

Yours always,

Swami Yogananda Giri

P. S. Please tell Mildred I will reply to her in my next letter. I am glad you are going to give me a surprise by coming here.

S.Y.

The Bancroft Hotel
Worcester, Mass.
November 8, 1923

Dear Doctor,

Infinite are the ways in which the Sly Eluder wants to test us. Anyway never mind I will be game to the occasion, and I am constantly asking Power from Him, that He might keep me surcharged with His Power to come out successfully thru this test. Don't forget He is your Father, infinitely kind to you more than anybody else. Forsake all, yet leave not His side.

Please forgive delay in sending this check as I did not know exactly how much money I would have left after you have cashed this check. Anyway do not forget I am with you, as God is. I will reach Boston tomorrow afternoon and would talk with you about the affair.*

Remember me to Brendoo, Bradford, Mildred and to yourself. With love everlasting.

> I remain very sincerely in the service of the Lord,
>
> Swami Giri Yogananda

P.S.   Herewith I enclose a check for $100.

---

*In October, 1923, Master had a short period of classes at the Hotel Bancroft in Worcester, Mass. and, at this time, asked Doctor for $1000 to go to New York to give a short series of lectures. This was the beginning of his lectures in this country.

The Waldorf-Astoria
New York, New York
November 23, 1923

Dear Doctor Lewis,

Words fail to express what you have done for Sat-Sanga.* Babaji, Lahiri Mahasaya and my Master's hands I see working through yours. You have inspired me. You have been the golden instrument of God's Touch—to manifest His Work. You have shown to me again that God helps when everybody fails.

And with the Almighty's strength I humbly bless you, that may He be pleased to give you more power, instill in you immortal nectar realization. May He give you unceasing faith and fulfill your desires and make you prosperous in every way.

My heart is shining with power as it never was, that God has selected such an unworthy nothingness like me to do His Work. Your spirit is with me—the real you is now coming in the limelight. Be not afraid child of the Eternal Lightning. March on with unperturbed steady steps—elbowing thru a million darknesses. Why what is body, what is this passing show—they are gone —but the candles that you are lighting and burning in your Father's house, will show you your path here and hereafter.†

---
*Illustrating the Master's handwriting, a copy of the first page of this letter is included on page 56.

† "The only reality is in God and our oneness with Him. Our Master and founder has pointed this out most wonderfully in a letter which he wrote to me; I value this letter as perhaps the greatest letter he has written to me, because the truth which he has pointed out in the letter aroused me so that I made the effort to rise above this outward consciousness and delusion and know that I was not that, but I was one with the Eternal Father, as each and every one of us is.

This letter written to me does not apply only to me, but applies to each and every one of us. Let us read it. This was written November 23, 1923, a

Sat-Sanga had a splendid reception last afternoon—the greatest demonstration of God's Work was given. The movie and cameramen were going away because of the rain and the clouds but just a few minutes before our arrival the supreme force dispersed the clouds and brought the sun out and as a result motion pictures etc. are to be released tonight all over the country. Herein I enclose what is going to be released and what came out in the Tribune.

Some have registered to take the courses without hearing my lecture. God's Hand is working through everything. Mrs. ___ came to see me and promises to help me in everything. New York has received Sat-Sanga in a wondrous way. I can speak no more.

How is Mildred, she was so nice last time I met her. How are you? Stand by God and His Servant and you will see His Hand working.

With infinite love to you all.

Affectionately yours,

Swami Yogananda Giri

---

long time ago, but I have found throughout these years that the words which he has written have not changed. They have become more real to me, I have tried to find flaws in his writings. I have been unable to do so, and that is why I give them to you. What he says applies to every one of us. This is part of his letter: 'Be not afraid Child of Eternal Lightning. March on with unperturbed steady steps—elbowing thru a million darknesses. Why what is body, what is this passing show—they are gone—but the candles that you are lighting and burning in your Father's house, will show you your path here and hereafter.'

Can there be any greater words than those? Don't get discouraged. Keep on meditating, and the candles that you are lighting in the Eternal Light of God will be there always to guide you, until finally you are one with the great light of the Infinite. Such are the words of the Master. They are worth listening to and following." — Dr. Lewis, referring to his letter, at the San Diego Church, January 25, 1959.

P.S. Important

Why don't you both come in a day. Please do come the day before Christmas and stay overnight in Waldorf. Come in your car. That will save a lot and we will see all New York. Please bring Mildred surely. You do not know how I will miss you tomorrow. Yet your spirit will be with us, your loyalty to truth will be with us. Please do come. Please come I mean seriously. The automobile expenditures [of renting] are horrible so I ask you to come by auto. You will enjoy staying here. I have a suite with four beds. You can sleep in my room and Mildred can live in the other. No extra expenditure. You will surely enjoy. We will get you Hindu food from Hindu restaurant and also good American food here. Do come. Do come. Do come.

With love,

Swami Yogananda

Hotel Pennsylvania
New York, New York
December 10, 1923

Dear Mildred,

... Please remember one thing, Sat-Sanga does not depend on anyone's mistakes, it is grounded in truth and its doctrines should be received as such. I invite constructive criticism, but ruthless public criticism simply for the love of it is against the laws of even simple friendship.*

Once more listen to the call of God, and pour your heart and soul for God's work. Imagine, if your heart received from here, inspiration and criticism, how much more would you have gained and benefited. *"Judge ye not others that ye be judged."*

Please do not do things and create circumstances thru hasty judgements, which will be beyond my power to repair.

Let me find you when I go to Boston with your angelic attitude which you once in a while show—let the virus, the inharmonious spirit that disturbs your own peace be removed, and let Sat-Sanga be made alive with your newer expressions during my absence. I write all this for your good and good of Sat-Sanga. Sat-Sanga is for you, I am its lawyer because my interests are identified with it at present—time will come when I shall not be a slave to any organization and will not pay heed to killing criticism, for I don't think those disturb me personally at all. Sat-Sanga is your larger home, larger field for your joyous play, I am building that for you, if you disturb it, remember you jeopardize your own interests.

I lecture 3 days beginning from tomorrow in this hotel. Great things are happening, and do not forget to give me

---

*Paramahansa Yogananda often remarked that he appreciated Mildred Lewis' forthrightness: "She's not afraid to tell me the truth."

a curry when I go there. Hoping to see you in best spirits. With blessings to you, Doctor, Brenda and Bradford.

>Very Sincerely Yours,
>
>Swami Giri Yogananda

Hotel Pennsylvania
New York, N. Y.
December 13, 1923

Dear Doctor and Mildred,

With our little faith even God has again demonstrated to us that He is with us. Do not ever forsake His side — believe we must if we want to seek Him. The devotee refuses to disbelieve.

I got Mildred's letter, and was very glad, I wished I had not sent the letter I sent you — I wrote that in a moment's agony. My love and joy for you people was at its height when I heard that terrible criticisms were going on before [others] and I nearly cried when I heard this. I thought, what is this God, it was so easy to create confidence in children but how difficult here. Please try to see things just as I felt and trust me I am telling facts as they are. If we don't trust one another just at one word, one saying, where will the world go?

I think amidst true friends, frankness is best, even if it is hurtful. I think sincerity and openmindedness which you possess are the best remedy for all misunderstandings. I will follow the principle as long as my God remains with me.

Now please henceforth make a solemn vow not to be disturbed by these trifling things, raise your souls above them, pity people who constantly delve in it. Make a vow that our love will never be questioned by our hearts nor be disturbed by anything or anybody else. That is too sacred to be disturbed in this way.

This is not the time to be downhearted — please show your spirits and keep me encouraged when I am giving everything body, mind, voice, sleep for you all. Forget all about it which was the result of misunderstandings and not motives on both sides, and unite your efforts to bring the Boston Festival successful in your absence. God is doing wonderful things here. I had packed houses every night here, students are coming in spite of Christmas.

This is the time to rejoice and not to weep or be vexed — Babaji's word is on the road to fulfillment. Gird up your loins and forget this trifling matter both of you, and remember the love for you behind the letter. ...

Let me see when I go to Boston your smiling faces beaming with God's smiles and joy and your hands busy with God's work thru Sat-Sanga.

With love to Bradford and Brenda and to you both,

> I remain very sincerely ever always,
>
> Swami Yogananda Giri

New York, New York
December 23, 1923

Dr. M. W. Lewis
18 Field Road
Arlington, Mass.

Love and Blessings, to you, Mil, children. Have sent your presents today.

SWAMI

Hotel Pennsylvania
New York, New York
February 8, 1930

Dear Mil,

It was sweet of you to remember me and remind me of the trip to California. All things are possible unto the Lord, if we are persistent enough. Results won't come of themselves, we have to bring them. Please use every ounce of your brain energy in making plans and putting them into action. Send thousands of literatures thru the medium of blue books etc.

I am really very very sorry not to be able to see Brad and Bren. How are they? Do they remember me?

Yoga is scientific contact of soul with God I often say, but with my progress on the spiritual path I am realizing more than ever that reverence is a great factor in salvation. I am trying to cultivate it and it is making my life sweet and carefree, free from any trace of egoism that might have lurked.

How is your meditation?

With my blessings and good wishes,

Very Sincerely yours,

Swami Yogananda Giri

The Bellevue Stratford
Philadelphia, Pa.

June 9, 1924

Dear Doctor,

Received your letter and telegram. I had been extremely busy. Please tell Mil I enjoyed the sandwich more than the cherries, for therein was something from both of you which the cherries hadn't and which can not be bought. I refused to buy cherries the night before and several times, because of their cost, and was overjoyed to receive them in time.

Please write to me at once, what house you mean to sell or rent. If it is your own house, please just rent it and don't sell now. Do not sell your home at 24 Electric Ave. You might rent it.

I am glad dear Doctor, you are working for God. Never before I was such as I am now, every day I am seeing His miracle. All those that will meekly come with me, they will see His work also. After all that is the only thing which is lasting. I have forgotten all little things in His work which is marching wonderfully. I am doing for you all and His children and nothing else. That was and ever shall be my pleasure.

Please meditate, concentrate on developing Sat-Sanga which is Babaji's work and God's. God helps those that help others materially and spiritually. Cast aside all fears, He is guiding you in everything. Feel your Father is with you, knows all your needs and would look after you (since you can't breathe without Him). Don't limit yourself by desires then you only get so much and nothing more. But if you want Him you have everything.

With love and blessings to you, Mildred and children.

Very sincerely yours,

Swami Yogananda

Write soon by Special Delivery, c/o 83 Walnut Ave., Merchantsville, N. J.

Hotel Pennsylvania
New York, New York
January 7, 1924

Dear Doctor,

Very glad to receive your letter. I like the pamphlets, they are nicely got up. I am very glad to hear of the response, too. I am glad Mildred likes the work.

I am very sorry that I have to put you in so much trouble. Don't be impatient dear Doctor just when the fruition is coming. Do I understand that you are going to borrow for the work $800 over and above the $500 you promised to give (of which $200 you have already paid to my bank). Well thank you extremely for your saving the life of the work, which has been founded and brought back after so much struggle. I think you are right in your suggestion of printing 3000 Yogoda. But I want to know right away how long it will take to print 3000 and whether $165 would be taken from $800 plus $500 or $1300 or $300 plus $200 (already deposited in my bank). Please let me know the rate of interest and the terms of payment (whether monthly or quarterly in what amount).

The Lecture Committee meets Friday and will arrange definitely about the lectures which I am going to give. I am trying utmost to [do] my duty, rest lies with God and the faith of you all. Please remember the broth must reach the stomach of the invalid person before he can feel strength. You can not ask him, if he feels strong or not, until and unless the broth reaches his stomach. So results will come when we sow the seeds — we have to take certain prospective most hopeful chances. It is impossible to judge the fruit when one sows a seed.

I am very glad the way you have started things just hold on to it—only don't back up or everything will be a huge farce. Impatience—be banished to the land of dreams.

With all my love to you all.

Very Sincerely yours,

Swami Yogananda

Hotel Pennsylvania
New York, New York
March 4, 1924

Dear Mil,

I am in receipt of your letter. Just the night before I received your letter I sat one hour telephoning to you from 1 A.M.—2 A.M. or a little later without any response. Really I feel awfully for you. Please do not think I have forgotten you all. I am praying to the Lord and it is in His power to act. Anyway, please don't give up courage. I phoned instruction which I hear you are minutely following. I don't know what you swallowed. Don't take cold or sour stuff. Eat tapioca and milk and eggs if you like. You must keep yourself nourished. Don't starve and please brick up and don't be too sensitive or suggest yourself with sickness or nausea. Please take regular walks and try to ride with windows of your car open. Don't stay in bed all the time if you can possibly avoid. I pray earnestly to God for your speedy recovery which I hope will be very soon.

My love and blessings to Brenda, Brad, you and Doctor. Please write to me daily about your state.

Very Sincerely yours,

Swami Yogananda Giri

Hotel Pennsylvania
New York, New York
April 26, 1924

Dear Mil and Doctor,

Thank you Mildred for remembering and resurrecting me on the Easter occasion. I am just passing through the whirlwind of work. They are giving a farewell dinner Tuesday night consisting of 60 students at $6.00 a plate in this hotel. A great effort is being made to make it a success. Unprecented things are happening—the Spirit of God, Babaji, Lahiri Mahasaya is moving your people. We are packing. I give 6 lectures in Philadelphia, 6 in the big and 2 in the small Psychology Clubs.

How is your work going? Falter not—carry on everything with incessant labor. Have faith and manifest faith in your action—and you will see God. I am growing every day, every day I am making fresh victories of myself—why can't you, surely you can. The great joy that comes in doing God's work unselfishly.

How are Brad and Bren, yourself and Mil? My blessing and love to you all. Do not make it a point not to write if I don't. My spirit is everywhere. It pleases me to hear from you all. I am very very very busy from 9 A.M. to 2 A.M.

Very sincerely yours,

Swami Yogananda Giri

June 24, 1924

Dear Doctor and Mil,

I cannot tell you how I enjoyed last time your beautiful silent kindness towards me. Never a question arose in my heart ever since I met you both, as to how you feel towards me. I know it and ever hereafter shall know it. I will never question it. After a long time the ride with you seemed so familiar, so natural, full of the most enjoyable sweetness. We can find better cars, better scenes, better automobiles, better rides, but not better joys which we had together in that particular ride.

It sometimes becomes very hard for me to rebuke Mildred, knowing what she feels within. I know and you know, how dearly God has grown our friendship.

With love to you both and the children.

Very Sincerely yours,

Swami Yogananda

P. S.

All the time feasting on Nature's scenes and drinking her Great Nectar. Every minute He is with me. Day and night slip by unnoticed. Be in God and Om. Now is the time.

POSTCARD
Vancouver, B. C.
September 6, 1924

Dr. M. W. Lewis
24 Electric Avenue
West Somerville, Mass.

Reached here safely (160 miles from Seattle). Large Hindu temple and 800 of them live here. You would have enjoyed seeing it.

Starting for Alaska on the 9th of September and back on the 22nd in Seattle where I stay to lecture.

Truth is our goal. Perseverance, love, steadiness leads to it.

With blessings and love to you all,

Very sincerely,

S. Yogananda

Hotel Anchorage
Anchorage, Alaska
September 18, 1924

Dear Doc and Mil,

Reached here safely at last through the several hundred mile long garden of snow-capped green mountains laid on the barren sea. I came from Seward by train. I saw glaciers by sea and land. The scenery is almost equal to Kashmir. Alaskan beauty can rightfully compete with Kashmir mountains and lotus lakes.* Wish you all had been here.

I am carrying with me new found beauties of God found in Nature.

Let only God Consciousness reign between us, let the everlasting spiritual tie be stronger than ever. It is never too late, if we try again and again. Kindliness, devotion, loyalty to God and your path lives forever. Let the good always dazzle before your eyes. Let darkness go. Love harmony. Boston is dear to me and ever shall be naughty or good it might be. Boston needs Sat-Sanga more than ever. Let my dear memories in Boston thrive, let my soul's confidence in the goodness of you all grow.

Let your hearts welcome the truth and you will find me always there to help you, to help you more than you ever dreamed. But doubt not when God tries you. Keep your abiding faith.

---

*In the premier issue of *East-West,* Nov–Dec 1925, Swami said of Alaska, "If it were possible to hold a beauty contest of all Nature's grandeurs and scenes of loveliness, it would be difficult to choose between Alaska and her Hindu sister Kashmir for the Queen's throne. If regal Kashmir with her floating gardens and lotus lakes, guarded all around by snow-crowned kingly ranges of the Himalayas, is the 'epitome of the world,' as the geographers say, then Alaska alone is worthy to vie with her for beauty and diversity of scenic glory."

With love to Brad and Bren and blessings and best wishes to you both.

Very sincerely yours,

S. Yogananda

———————

POSTCARD

c/o General Delivery
Seattle, Washington
September 25, 1924

Dear Doc and Mil,

Reached at last very near to our destination. We crossed the continent. Most delightful trip. I will never go back to train.

No matter what happens in the work, please do not forget my relation with you, I mean the Divine one. Keep that unconditioned untarnished. Life is short. Culture harmony, devotion, loyalty to the path and your spiritual friend. You will find peace everlasting. Never lose faith. My good will and care will forever protect you.

S. Yogananda

Over 5000 miles we traveled went over Pike's Peak in our car. Wish you both saw this wonderful place and were here. Very Sincerely.

Seattle, Washington
October 14, 1924

Dear Doctor and Mil,

Do you know that every morning at 7 o'clock I send a spiritual message to you for your highest spiritual unfoldment and success in life? Do your own part. The spiritual seed given to you in the shape of lessons will bear fruits only if you moisten it daily and regularly with the water of patient practice. Protect your little growing spiritual plant from the insects of doubt, and physical or mental idleness.

You will be glad to know that I reached Seattle on September 3rd after an automobile trip of over 5,000 miles. On September 9th I went to Anchorage, Alaska on a wonderful 26 day trip.* I lectured at Denver to 2,500 people in the city auditorium and had a large class. A Denver Sat-Sanga is established. After my return from celestial Alaska, I lectured to more than 2000 people in the Masonic Auditorium in Seattle. A Seattle Sat-Sanga is in view. Your brothers and sisters are increasing.

Don't forget I am coming to you again with a new inspiration which our beautiful America has given to me. Do not forget Christ sleeps in you and the teachers of India are trying to help you. The world needs you just as they need me. Spiritually prepare yourself for the regular practices of what I taught you. In order to give, you must possess.

With blessings and prayers eternal, I remain,

Sincerely yours,

Swami Yogananda

---

*Aboard the S. S. Admiral Evans.

> Up to 29th Oct.
> c/o Multnomah Hotel
> Portland, Oregon

Dear Doctor and Mil,

Received your very kind letter. I have been mentally replying to you a dozen times without being physically able to do so. The enclosed card will show. I am still giving lessons to a fairly big class. I lectured to 2000 people each day.

Henceforth, God will create in us the greatest spiritual relationship that ever existed. Between us will exist positive thoughts of kindliness and heaven untrammeled by negative thoughts at all. I am experiencing a newer phase of life. God has been very kind to me. So he will be kind to you. Never did you bring so much goodness out of me as you have done. What spiritual help you want, that is yours. More than that, time will tell, that if God ever gives the opportunity materially I will show what I can do for my little Bradford and Brenda.

I have found the law of love and reciprocal goodness are the strongest ties, the greatest impelling forces, that make us responsible to one another. That's why the material binding is futile and meaningless specially where there is a spiritual tie. The organization is greatly indebted to you materially and this it will repay a thousand-fold. And if perchance, if its fate is otherwise, still the goodwill that you have created in me, will forever cry in the Divine ether, for you, for your welfare and success and you shall see God will fulfill all your wants and the wants of your family, more than you expect.

A life without trouble and vicissitudes is tasteless, insipid. Troubles come, let them come, they will be your stepping stones for your upward climb. I am very glad that you are anchoring on the Infinite One. He will never fail you.

I am very glad to hear that you got a place of rest. It is strange that your father in spite of being an upright man has not the power to show it in his actions.* He hides behind his weakness. It is pitiable. Someday he will realize what he is doing by treating you this way. Someday I want to talk to him. I must tell him squarely what he is doing. In the meantime, if you can talk to him, it will be mighty good.

About me—now I am in Portland as you can see on the card enclosed. Two hundred people walked away. I talked in the Assembly Hall. There is great enthusiasm everywhere. More than 1100 people were present. In Seattle according to the size of the city I had 2000 people each day in the Masonic Auditorium.

I write this letter from Portland—the rest of it. I do not know how days and nights are passing. Please write to me til 29th Oct. c/o Multnomah Hotel, Portland, Oregon. After that write me c/o General Delivery, San Francisco, California.

Mildred and you both meditate deeper and deeper. Every morning I remember you and think of those dear days of our travel together.

With my blessings to you both and much love to Brendu and Bradak. Ask Brad if he remembers me. Please let me know if you received the things I sent to you from Seattle.

With my best blessings again.

Very Sincerely yours,

S. Yogananda

---

*In October of 1935, Paramahansaji wrote the following to Doctor and Mrs. Lewis, "Each person is by Divine right given independence to do as he pleases, so even God can't help an individual if he chooses to do wrong."

Palace Hotel
San Francisco, California
November 19, 1924

Dear Doctor and Mil,

Received your most kind letter. I am sorry that Minie* couldn't use the slippers. Anyway you had a fine time Mil didn't you? All right Minie I shall send you something very good—have you any special choice—then write—anything you shall have it. I am glad for Brad and Bren. Please give my love to them.

Do you know your Swami has consecrated his limbs, blood, flesh, comfort, life, energy, everything to His God's and Guru's work and to glorify you all. Everything turning out just as I expected. Everything shall turn out just as you expected too. Only keep the Infinite harmony that is between us. This is of God and in God it shall rest. Please cheer me once in a while with your kindness. There is no word which I can use for my busy work.

With my blessings always,

Sincerely yours,

Swami Yogananda

P.S. How is your meditation going Doctor?

---

*Doctor Lewis was known as "Minie" by his close friends.

Biltmore Hotel
Los Angeles, California
January 25, 1925

Dear Doctor,

I received your very delightful letter. I am glad to hear of your spiritual improvement. I perfectly realized about what you wrote. Please forgive me for this delay. I thank you for the patience with me. Please don't lose confidence. I have been bleeding and working for you all—Americans—Hindus all—for all your sisters and brothers of the world. This delay is due to your larger family's necessities, not mine. So please forgive. Tasks seem endless, bleeding unceasing, I have to be responsible, even though I bleed for you all. Things are going wonderfully, but expenses are heavy too. I am printing several books. Indeed just as I felt to come to Los Angeles like a meteor or a bombshell.

I had the Philharmonic Auditorium filled every night, 3000 people every night and some turned away. So I am giving another course of lectures. I had 450 students—after this Sat-Sanga is marching on.

God knows of all your good activities and help to the cause of which all of us are servants. My love and blessings to you both and Brad and Bren. Cannot tell you how busy I am.

With blessings,
Very sincerely yours,

Swami Yogananda

P. S.   I enjoy receiving your letters. Please thank Mil for her letter. Please both write. I am glad she is improving. I long for the curries at your place.

S.Y.

c/o Multnomah Hotel
Portland, Oregon
May 30, 1925

Dear Doctor,

I am glad at last you have remembered me. I was literally so busy it is impossible for me to keep up my correspondence with those that I love. I mentally think of you all but I can not write simply because of heavy daily correspondence that requires formal attention.

Anyway, how are you all? Moving along in the same familiar way. We must follow a path and it must quicken our movement in that. My life has become strangely busy, every night, except a few nights in a month I have to lecture.

There was a time when I tried to do good things to earn good opinions, but now life has offered me a new proposition. I do good things not goaded by the compelling whip of duty but with the sense of privilege. As God's child created in perfection nothing is due from me, or I have no duty. My only privilege is to please God and make use of the right discrimination, sympathy, etc. which God has given me. I like to do good to others because I have found in it my highest joy. I can do good to others in the sunshine of fame and in the darkness of adverse criticism. Serve I must, rain or shine, serve I must for that is my joy. That has been my life and I value all life's experiences. Meditate unceasingly, that's the only way to directly reach the Spirit.

Please realize I have to write books, answer myriads of letters and prepare lectures. I am alone but I have many friends. I like to hear from them but it is very difficult for me to write to them. Those good old days are never to be forgotten. Going to lecture in Portland in June.

Please let me know about Brad, Bren, Mil and yourself. With lots of blessings to you all,

>Very Sincerely yours,
>
>S. Yogananda

                    Sentinel Hotel
                    Yosemite National Park
                    California

                    [Before 1926]

Dear Minott and Mildred,

   At last reached here. It is all snow here, just like Boston. Couldn't go there so had to bring Boston to me. Ah Christmas is near. I hope you have got the little things I sent you. Enclosed is for Bradford's and Brenda's bank, which I hope you have already started. Bodily I will be away but not in Spirit. On New Year's night when you eat keep an empty chair around the table in front of Minott—my spirit will be there.
   I reach Los Angeles January 2, Hotel Biltmore, Los Angeles.

   I am enjoying Yosemite, first resting after a big week in San Francisco.

   My blessings of Christmas for a new awakening in faith and meditation.

   With blessings and love to you all, Brad and Bren, your Mother, Grandpa and everybody I know.

                    Very affectionately,

                    Swami Yogananda

   I will miss you on Christmas night.

January 11, 1926

Dr. M. W. Lewis
24 Electric Avenue
West Somerville, Mass.

Dear Dr. Lewis,

During my last visit in Boston, I was pleased to hear about the little group gathering in your home, trying to preserve the spirit of Sat-Sanga. I have found in my other organizations in different cities it is very hard to keep a group together without a leader. All the members of a group sometimes want to be just leaders whether they have the power to become so or not. To be a leader is to be the least the servant of all. Then again the members of Sat-Sanga who have had a continuous training for five years ought to be able to harmonize together and preserve the spirit of Sat-Sanga thru their own efforts when we are away. It is everybody's own business to be better. The essence of the message of Sat-Sanga is self-development by self-effort and by contacting the Spirit within. That's the inner phase. Yet the outer phase of Sat-Sanga points out the necessity of creating a bodyguard of good company since materially one has to choose some sort of company.

Hence I am pleased very pleased that a little group, little hive but with lots of spiritual honey gather together. I find from experience that every organization, when denuded of a leader from India, must have a representative of his own, selected by his own spiritual intuition. That I think will eliminate the question of as to who should lead and prevent petty jealousies which are the canker that eats at the root of harmony from which an organization draws its very life.*

---

*In a letter dated December 15th, 1941, Paramahansa Yogananda wrote,

As I have observed your life and faithfulness to Yogoda practices and my teachings and loyal friendship to me, I have the pleasure to select you the present leader of the Boston Sat-Sanga group, and that the members of the said organization will cooperate with you on a basis of true rational friendship, harmony and perfect co-operation.

You with your co-workers may follow any plan to conduct the weekly meetings in your home, suited to the best needs and wishes of the majority. The final decision of matters concerning Boston Sat-Sanga will rest with you acting in co-operation with my wishes. Please have a regular organization, sending out invitation cards, inviting new members. You must look to both qualitative and numerical strength of your organization. I would very much like that you affirm every week something from the Scientific Affirmations and the Bhagavad Gita. By affirmations I mean you should read one line followed by the repetition of same by others loudly, until a verse is finished. ...

Please read my letter to all the members of the organization, and preserve this to show to anyone who might ask you about my wishes for the Boston group. My teacher obeys God—I harmonize with my teacher's wishes—and all those who will harmonize with my wishes, obey not me but my teacher, my Guru and the great God.

With blessings to you all again and may the New Year bring to you all New Realizations.

Very Sincerely Yours,

Swami Yogananda

"Unless you concentrate on good and seeking only good — gravitating to negative things in organization would drive you crazy. Only by seeing good have I laughed and preserved my sanity. Organization life is different and peace is found if only concentration is on good."

Hotel Pennsylvania
New York, New York
Feb. 8, 1926

Dear Doctor,

I am very pleased to receive your letter. I am very sorry to hear of Mr. Mills. I fully believed you could have helped him if he didn't transfer the charge to the sub-conscious mind. Strange to say I had strong premonition of Mr. Mills' trans-ether flight to the freer regions.

Everything is difficult in this world, but victory is only to those that persevere to the last. I will soon send an exclusive list of prominent New Yorkers, which I have received by chance and without cost. Please remind me again about it.

I am silently working, and I do not wish to trouble you with my worries—and no use informing until something definite happens—only this much things are progressing to my expectations. I am doing my utmost—the rest lies with God.

Please do not expect results without pushing Yogoda and planning for it. Brain labor always pays. Please send thousands of literature according to exclusive mailing list. Results are bound to follow. We have to cover a wide area. All for God and God for All. I am enjoying Him more than ever—no distractions though heavy responsible duties.

I miss you all very much. With my love to you, Brenda and Brad. How is your meditation? Remember 2 or 3 years of 1/24 hour of daily meditation is only little. Go deeper intensely. Always through strain and stress always remain by God's Side.

Very Sincerely yours,

Swami Yogananda Giri

Hotel Pennsylvania
New York, New York
April 14, 1926

Dear Doctor,

Just yesterday came from Cuba via Philadelphia. Your telegram came late. But I did best what I could do by prayers and as much as her karma would allow. Though I did not write to you knowing your Mother was sick, yet mentally I was active all to my best ability. You have not yet informed me about her. Please let me know all details.

Couldn't you and Mildred sometimes come over here— Oh that would be more than wonderful. Lectures start from the 18th of April to 26th inclusive except Monday and Saturday.

My love to children and you both blessings always.

Very sincerely yours,

Swami Yogananda

Hotel Pennsylvania
New York, New York
May 10, 1926

Dear Boston Students:

I was very happy to receive your glad tidings per Dr. Lewis who breathed your united spirit, love and kindness.

Qualitatively improve yourselves by deepening your efforts in concentration, numerically try to grow by interesting a friend at least in the cause and serve all with kind words and your all. Keep your eyes fixed on harmony and progressive activity and unlimited faith in God's Limitless Power.

Blessings and Eternal Good Wishes to you all.

Very sincerely yours,

Swami Yogananda

> The Plaza
> Fifth Avenue at 58th Street
> New York, New York
> May 25, 1926

Dear Doctor,

I hope you all are faring well, meditating and progressing. Let us henceforth always more and more concentrate on the spiritual relationship that exists between us and emphasize less and lesser material transactions. The material will take care of itself. Give my love to Bradford and Brenda. My blessings to you both.

> Very sincerely yours in Om,
>
> Swami Yogananda

P. S. Just stopped here for a night, going back to Philadelphia, this afternoon. I am working incessantly for God and all.

S.Y.

---

c/o Gibson Hotel
Cincinnati, Ohio
Oct. 9, 1926

Dear Doctor Lewis,

How is everything going—you ask about your faith. Your faith is practical enough but it could be better. Faith is acquired by having faith when there is cause to lose it. Faith has to be cultured. Still one's faith applied to others problem—as in your mother's case has two sides. Faith is the window thru which the Divine Light shines. None wishes more than the Divine Light itself to shine thru the window of our faith to give us health, prosperity and Bliss. But thru long-continued wrong living and forgetfulness of God we close the windows of faith and the Divine Light is shut out producing sickness and lack. Your mother's window was shut—we tried to open it with the help of God—it opened a little but there were others who held it down too—your mother.

Karma also held it down so the Divine Light could not shine thru. The Divine Light itself with all of its willingness was powerless—because it has given freedom to its Cosmic and Karmic laws which govern human life. Losing faith means closing windows. What you see you believe easily—but God suggests Himself enough as in Nature, "Why He talked enough to me thru the budding mouth of the rose and His petalled cheeks blushed in joy to see me thru the sunshine." Those that believe in spite of everything they gradually see the Super law work.

We are like children yet asking this and that from the Divine Mother and sometimes when She can not give us something because of Her laws—we doubt Her or Her power. But keep on meditating and there shall come one day, when the veil will be torn—all the veil of laws created by Maya will be gone and we will be free standing face to face with our Divine Mother—then we will see Her protection working behind the physical, untrammelled, uninterruptedly. Then nothing but the breeze of Immortality and perennial Joy will sustain us.

Work for that—it is a long walk—but keep busy and someday, suddenly, the end will be reached. Don't look how far you have to go, but how little you have to walk today—how little you have to meditate deeply today. It is because many people neglect being deeply devoted in their daily meditation that they feel the distance too great. Give up hopes, fears, desires, cry for the Divine Mother every time after meditation, "Divine Mother this day is passed, I have not seen Thee yet."

My love and blessings to you, Mil, Brad and Bren. In spite of terrible distractions I am find Him more and more. With campaign work and students increasing my work is increasing.

With love I remain,

Very Sincerely yours,

Swami Yogananda

P.S. Your proposal about moving away from Electric Avenue looks ripe to me and if living on one floor is helpful to Mildred it is alright to do so at once. You have waited long. Hurry then—thinking of the great God while doing so.

Love,

S. Y.

Denver, Colorado
August 19, 1926

Dear Doctor and Mil,

Received your kind letter and appreciate your remembering me. Many things transpired ever since I landed in Boston in 1920. You know how I suffered mutely all for Sat-Sanga. You know too well as to how I have suffered because of the small way in which the organization was started. Here the psychology is quite different — even Truth has to go in an organized way, otherwise it is not only not received but rejected, and even slighted. Then again if you test a truth amidst a small minority, and then you don't know of the lasting spiritual qualities of that minority — then it is doing injustice to Truth. (I do not mean to doubt your spirituality or some others, nor have I desire to include you in the minority). I suffered, wept tears just because I did not know the law of organization and presentation of Truth. But some of the people of Boston spared no pains to take advantage of this fact and even slighted Truth for my ignorance.

I prayed to God and when all human efforts had failed, His strength came. He injected new courage into me and I launched into the unknown. I have loved God above everything and hope to do so always. I prayed to Him to take me away from Boston, if I was not needed. He answered me in the negative. He wanted me, that's why you remember how I dashed myself on impossibilities and sure-failing schemes from the human point of view. You played a great part of it—and remember the night before I started for New York with the troupe you felt God move your heart in your R & V Knight car. I shall never deny it and whenever you will want me to declare it I will do so from the housetops. Instead I shall always love you as one of the dearest things of my heart. You know it and I want you never to lose faith in that. For if that is false, God is false, Truth is false, Love is false, I am false and money is greater than all these.

Now then I ask you another question—have you ever found me acting with any selfish motive, other than the good of Sat-Sanga and the public? I hope you can never dream otherwise. It is useless to make the old repetition that I have no ambition for money for Self, and that money that came from India was sufficient to support me.

I believe in honest organization that is done wholly for God. Business is good if carried on honestly. But I have realized lately that business may apply to broad big organizations as well as to a small family. But it is true that if we do even partly small family business in the name of big philanthropic business it would be thought otherwise. Interest of the organization always ran supreme in my mind. As a drowning man catches at a straw I sought an outlet to establish Sat-Sanga teachings. ...I knew that spiritual as you are—the interest of Sat-Sanga would ring deeper in your heart than the interest of your family. ...I consider souls more valuable than organizations or anything else.

I do not know why God's test comes so hard upon me—a few months back you would have been glad to get rid of the Mail Course. You thought we could not run it. Then again without a wide publicity it would share the fate of Boston organization. Now the question is do you want me to go on as things went on or do you want me to act otherwise? ...

Then again, you know how unfortunate my efforts were in Boston just because I did not know the law of organization. I am the same Yogananda who coaxed sixty people to listen to him and hardly he could get that number. Now he talks to up to 2000 people. I am unchanged, only I have got bigger scope to serve and work for your countrymen. I talked in Denver in the City Auditorium (bigger than Symphony Hall, Boston). I thank God for giving me experiences in Boston and I am satisfied.

I sincerely wish, henceforth, that God's work be done in God's way and no side track policy. I wish the same straight respectful relations with all my students. You will all then love the truth more. By familiarity you have loved me more than Truth. Harmony I can not create—I can sow the seeds, but the mental ground of disciples their own enthusiasm should take care of the rest.

I am starting for Yellowstone on the 21st or 22nd of August reaching in 4 days—with staying there about 4 or 5 days. Then start to Seattle to go perhaps to Alaska.

With my same old blessings for your highest all-round success and love to you both and children.

Very Sincerely yours,

Swami Yogananda

Hotel Pennsylvania
New York, N. Y.
January 2, 1927

Dear Doctor,

Words fail to express what I feel. The pleasant memory of Boston and Christmas with you is strong with me. Time is passing, events are coming and with infinite patience I am trying to do what is best.

I am superbly happy to know that you have a practical hand in the great work we have taken up. Remember Rome was not built in a day, and if you persevere and show your mettle of courage and persistency a little above the ordinary then and then only you will see things that are out of the ordinary.

Three Town Hall meetings are being arranged at the Committee's expense. Don't you think we should distribute "Yogoda" at the last meeting to all freely—it would mean much for people would understand more if they get a book along with my lecture. But at last something was done. The Committee at last took charge of 3 lectures to be delivered by me in Town Hall at their own expense. That they have shared this responsibility with me shows that God at last has done something.

Yet now we have to take a definite stand, and should be able to meet all situations with calmness and without worry. I told the Committee that Boston had hitherto looked after New York expenses. To which Mr. Hunsicker replied, "Of course we don't want Boston to look after our expenses." So the Committee forthwith took charge of the lectures, and they say they are going to fill the Town Hall. They meet tonight again. Two Committees have been appointed, one Lecture Committee, another Main Committee. Mr. Hunsicker has promised to send me to other places Chicago,

Cleveland etc.

Last night we had a great meeting. Something practical was done at last. There was a great debate last night. Things at times seemed to hang in the balance. At times it seemed, nothing would be accomplished. Besides the topics of my lecture in Town Hall has to be different. I haven't many books of Yogoda, the types are still preserved and reprinting them would not cost much. It has to be considered soon.

Harrah imagine once for all I haven't myself to think of arranging meetings for the good of all. Last night was the greatest meeting in the life of Sat-Sanga.

With my blessings and with big joy which I received this last Christmas.

I will keep you informed with latest developments, I remain,

Very sincerely yours,

Swami Yogananda

P. S.   Please give my love to Bradford and Brenda.

The Mayflower Hotel
Washington, D. C.

February 5, 1927

Dr. M. W. Lewis
253 Elm Street
Lewis Building, Davis Square
West Somerville, Mass.

Dear Dr. Lewis:

Your letter received with great joy. I am sorry not to have acknowledged the splendid Christmas gifts that were given to me. Please thank Brad and Bren for their wonderful choice and consideration of me.

Tell Mildred her prophesy came true, that some one of these days I'd see Cal (Calvin Coolidge). I did see him. I send an enclosed picture. In God's work here I have been progressive.

[Balance of letter missing.]

Hotel Statler
Buffalo, New York
May 6, 1927

Dr. M. W. Lewis
253 Elm Street
West Somerville, Mass.

Dear Dr. Lewis,

I was very happy to receive your nice letter together with the poem and essay which I am sending on to the Editor of East-West Magazine, to be used in the near future.*

Remember me to Mildred and the children.

With Blessings,

Swami Yogananda

---

*Throughout the years, Dr. Lewis contributed various articles, poems, and lectures to the magazine.

Colorado Springs, Colorado
August 1927

Dear Doctor,

Have been extremely busy. I made every attempt to go to Boston. I was all ready—ticket was bought but my telegram returned so I thought you were in Duxbury. Awfully sorry to have missed you. I long to see you. All I can say I will try henceforth, "Seeing is believing" is right.

Why didn't you send me a photo of your nice home. I have christened it in Spirit for my Spirit was there with you. Meditate deep and deeper—Dive deeply like a plummet of devotion until you reach the bottom of Divine Mother's Sea-breast.

Please receive my love and blessings and give them to the children and Mil.

With love eternal,
Very sincerely yours,

Swami Yogananda

Lowry Hotel
St. Paul, Minnesota
November 3, 1927

Dr. M. W. Lewis
253 Elm Street
Lewis Building
West Somerville, Mass.

Dear Dr. Lewis:

I received your letter of October 13th and am sorry that the telegram did not reach you. I expect to leave for St. Paul on Saturday and start a series of free lectures there on Sunday afternoon. You may reach me at the Hotel Lowry.

Do your best with the Hermitage. We must dispose of the property.*

With blessings to you all unceasingly. O how I long to see you all.

Very sincerely yours,

Swami Yogananda

---

*It was Paramahansaji's wish to dispose of the Waltham Hermitage.

The Lowry Hotel
St. Paul, Minn.
Nov. 14, 1927

Dr. M. W. Lewis
18 Field Road
Arlington, Mass.

Dear Doc,

I have received the bangle safely and thank you for your kindness in making and sending it on, also for looking up my speeches in Harvard Crimson.* The copy which you have made has not yet arrived but believe it will be along in a day or two.

O how I long to see you, Mil, Brad and Bren. You don't know—I shall not promise but I will try.

With love, blessings and prayers always,

Sincerely yours,

Swami Yogananda

---

*A publication of Harvard University.

Philadelphia, Pa.
No date

Dear Doctor,

I was very happy to receive your loving letter. Please know once I am a friend I will be so always. My love for you is unconditioned by any circumstance. ...

Well, it is my fate to get hit, crucified again and again. In human success or failure is not success or failure with God—bruised battered and fallen even then if once one thinks. "God my body can not move, but I have not given up I am mentally moving to Thy Shores." To that person when the Supreme test is really done and complied with, God comes—So don't give up. Hold on.

Please let me know about your health above all—I am praying continuously—I would take the exercises easy and cultivate mental whispers of devotion to God.

With love and unceasing blessings to you all.

Very sincerely yours,

Swami Yogananda

Hotel Everglades
Miami, Florida
January 25, 1928

Dr. M. W. Lewis
253 Elm Street
West Somerville, Mass.

Dear Doc,

I am glad to know that the little presents sent you for Christmas were so well received. With them were my best wishes.

I should very much have liked to have spent Christmas with you there, however, as that was impossible I did what was perhaps the next best thing—tried to express my feelings and have myself represented by means of the little gifts.

I certainly would be glad to have and cherish any little present or remembrance which you may have for me. If you send it right away, it will get to me by addressing it here to The Everglades Hotel. ...

Miami is a lovely city and as far as the city itself and the weather is concerned, one could not ask for better and I only wish you and those near and dear to you were here to enjoy it with me.

Blessings,

Swami Yogananda

New York, New York
March 19, 1928

Dear Doc,

Please try your utmost to get the enclosed letter into the newspapers if it has not already come out which I very much doubt. I shall greatly appreciate it.

I had such a wonderful time with you and Mil and the children.

Please pull all the wires you can to get this in the papers. Please do work hard for this if you ever worked hard for the cause—work fast.

O it was so good to be with you all. Infinite love and joy was revived—a new life I felt. O blessed ones of the Lord—you have all my blessings of my heart forever. Ask Brad and Bren if they think of me. Mildred was good—harmony crowns you all!

Love and Blessings to all,

Swami Yogananda

Yogoda Sat-Sanga Society
509 Fifth Avenue
New York, New York
May 10, 1928

Dear Doctor Lewis,

Please sign this document authorizing ___ with full authority for executing my Correspondence Course. Please sign the four copies before a notary public with two witnesses and send them to me.

I thank you very much for what you sent and I am deeply praying to right your conditions. Only the Great One can help.

> "I take these things away from thee
> That thou mayest receive them
> From my hands
> From me.

Be steady in storm and sunshine and His Light you will see shining fully behind the clouds and sunny circumstances.

With love,
Very Sincerely yours,

Swami Yogananda

May 23, 1929

Dear Doctor,

With a heavy heart I am starting for Mexico. When the sword of so many responsibilities hangs on my head, Dear Doctor we must fight the battle to the end. Your success in life is of deep concern as well as this work. I would not advise you wrongly though it is difficult to bear the cross. We all have to bear our crosses, the few who love to live for God and God's work. In this momentary dream of life when others are smiling with material dream (success) only to wake up in nightmare of suffering we must dream for God—hold ambition for God's work.

I would never have taxed you further if God did not already respond. Without your cooperation we will be soon in the same trial we were before. So please do not fail God at this hour. It may be very hard but please do it. Without your help great danger is in sight. We will fight our way to freedom.

And this is my request please learn to hold onto the hand of God when everything seems to discourage or destroy you. Please tell Mildred not to counteract my efforts to help you all.* For each person is a child of God and will strongly slip out consciously or unconsciously may have havocking effect—which may be too late to mend. When you do help God's work and have been helping do it willingly, gladly, smilingly casting all fear overboard.

---

*Sometimes Paramahansaji was strict with Mrs. Lewis, but he never doubted her loyalty, as he once wrote to Doctor: "You and I think in the same way along with Mildred when it comes to loyalty."

I am going and praying constantly and will bring blessings and prosperity by surprises so believe and act and God will never fail you. Behold He is with you with everything.

                        Very Sincerely yours,

                        Swami Yogananda

Monday—Havana

Dear Doctor,

Farther and farther I am moving away. I am in the same old Havana. So much wish you were all here. Cutting loose from everything—that's what I am doing—that I may consecrate myself to Him myself entirely. Meditation night and day—a part of it will reach you—meditate deeper than ever. Meditation is friendship with God. In meditation alone you hear His voice of peace—His loud talk of Infinite Assurance. Meditation is the net to catch the Divine Amphibian.

Have more faith—complain not—Bite more than you can in His Name—then chew it. Try more than you can and then do it.

Last of all remember—now is the time or never. Meditate deeply at night. Throw yourself at the feet of God. Steady coaxing is necessary. Sincere heart-call to make Him speak. Forget this dream of life—lo in the chamber of imagination—life is already filmed and finished. Don't wait, pray unceasingly for illumination and God's Love—lose not a minute. Don't be fed up by waiting hopes of this and that—eat God now—nourish yourself on eternity.

Love and all that I feel to you, Mil, Brad and Bren and all.

Very Sincerely,

Swami Yogananda

Mexico
July, 1929

Dear Mil,

Thank you for your kind letter. I appreciate it. Mexico so like India. Wish you all were here.

Met the president of Mexico. Great many developments. Took extensive movie films—came out fine. You will be glad to see them.

Do not forget God's work and He will never forget you.

Please write to L.A.—reaching there next Saturday, July 27.

Blessings to you, Brad, Bren unceasingly.

Very sincerely yours,

Swami Yogananda

Chapala, Mexico
July 21, 1929

Dear Doctor,

Thank you very much for the bangle, you certainly sent it to the party in need on time. It saved lots of trouble.

I wonder if you received my card which I sent you from Mexico long ago. I would have so much liked to hear from you. Are you not feeling right because of my last request? Dear Doctor there are few in this world who feel for God's work as they do for their own. Few bleed for Him. Few assume responsibility for His work as they do for their own. You always have been one of those few—that's why you were asked to share the burden at the most crucial hour. There are few like you who feel for God's work. If some like you and us don't do our best how will Ignorance Satan's Kingdom be destroyed?

[Second page missing]

3880 San Rafael Avenue
Los Angeles, California
November 14, 1929

Dear Doctor,

Thank God for saving us when thousands lost. Anyway, things must come back—only hold quiet and tight. God certainly has acted through you—in future unless I sufficiently concentrate I would not undertake to ask you to buy. Anyway know this for certain, whatever trials come to us—what is mine is yours too—and time will bring to you untold opportunities and enough prosperity to you to enable you to pursue your spiritual career. Only doubt not at the mysterious ways of God. At last I have found what I was seeking—wish dear ones you were here to enjoy with me this Heaven. ...

What is life without real joy and God. Why slave all life to die of worries and distraction. Oh God is with me all the time and I so much wish to meditate with you here. I very much like to bring you here sometime and see this place yourself, what it is and how it is developing. I am meditating and in Him all the time. Oh what joy.

Please give my love and unceasing blessings to Mil, Brad and Bren and to you.

Very sincerely yours,

Swami Yogananda

Fort Nelson Hotel
Louisville, Kentucky

Dr. Lewis Loved One,

Thank you for what help came. It tided over somewhat. I grieve not for what I get not—for I desire nothing. I only try for His work as others try for their own.

I had to tear myself from Boston. Lovely beyond dreams I enjoyed your dear home. Think how fortunate you are whereas others lost their home with greater money. Divine Mother's play is wondrous and subtle. She beats us that we may cling to Her. She is very clever. I think I know all Her Infinite tricks to make us forget Her.*

With a Very Happy New Year and multi-blessings and love to you, Mildred, Bradford and Brenda and all Yogodans.

Very Sincerely Yours,

S. Yogananda

---

*Dr. Lewis often referred to this letter as "Tricks of Divine Mother."

3880 San Rafael Avenue
Los Angeles, California
January 21, 193[?]

Dear Doctor,

Received your letter. Please do not get so discouraged. There are people in far worse plight than you or me. It is only we should always compare our ill-times with worse times of others—then we will find how fortunate we are.

Your health was bad once—it became well, you should think of that. It is bad now it can be well again. If you are despondent, give up hope—how can you receive help? The Divine can only help when we can unceasingly uncomplainingly keep the window of faith open. It is our age-long unfaith which shades our soul-opening and prevents the ever-shining Light to get through. This shade can only be kept open by unceasing faith in spite of reverses in everything. Nearer you reach God trials seemingly appear very severe—but the one who steadily believes and thus deserves God's direct action and help will find some magic wand dissolving all menacing mountains of testing tribulations. I have found this many times. Why don't you have patience? Why don't you remember how God had helped you when matters could be worse.

1. God gave you a sea beach home.

2. God relieved you of indigestion.

3. God gives you peace through meditation every day which millions, millionaires have not.

4. God has given you a faithful wife.

5. God saved us from a crash in which all may have been lost.

Instead of brooding over imaginary losses you should put your shoulders to the wheel and help me advertise. Doing away with everything I am staking everything in advertising. The old slow way of advertising must be forsaken. The world is our field for spreading the message and getting the where-with-all to do so.

I know like Smith Brothers (Cough Drops) we are two spiritual souls bound together to propel this work to great heights. Others will sit, laugh and watch. You must come to my help in this matter, I told you long ago, yet our momentary blindness took us to work the wrong investment. Instead of brooding over imaginary losses, come to my help and I will show you how to attract financial freedom and with it spiritual freedom. But financial freedom can bring spiritual freedom only to those who are constantly trying to be spiritually free and are on the watch. Otherwise financial freedom is the cause of bondage, harbinger of all false happiness and sense pleasures. A certain amount of worries (if they don't get too fresh) are stimulants to our soul. Dear Doctor please write to me in detail typed clearly all your ailments and I will do my best immediately.

And if my body lasts this much I can tell you, we will enjoy financial freedom if you co-operate with me without fear. If it had been only my freedom I would not have bothered—I would have taken shelter under a tree.

Dear Doctor it is for the very freedom you seek I want you to co-operate with me financially heart and soul—and you will see the sure results. Remember your donations in the beginning how much they have done—and a few thousand more with work so much advanced as the foundation will positively bring the desired result—Freedom. Besides dear one besides financial freedom—many other freedoms have to be sought—disease, accidents, misfortunes, separations and lastly death. You have to work fast. Of course, financial freedom plays an important part and spiritual freedom plays the most important part—for then you are free when even in a cage.

> "Stone walls and diseases do not a prison make
> Nor iron bars a cage
> Minds innocent, God protected take
> That for a Heaven, a Hermitage."

It is because I feel entire responsibility of your life that is why I ask you to help me—to help you and all. So please do not stop the steady flow of advertisements which I have started. Do not cut off the vital vein which is rushing towards us to free us. I have invested heavily already in advertisements—results are very hopeful—please feed this vein. Bear a little difficulty now—but do constantly feed this vein, feed it—this is the trial of Satan that I have to ask you for help. For God wants a true son (to be tested) who is worthy to help now. I know none of the idle rich will help now. Read the history of great movements—it is only the most sincere ones who have saved the boat in time of storm.

Please understand and be assured that this is our greatest dash for spiritual freedom. We are striving to have financial freedom that we might attain spiritual freedom ourselves and those of others.

Trust me doubt me not and I will show you the way to freedom. Boundless love and everything that is mine is at your service. With love and unceasing blessings to you, Mil, Brad and Bren.

Yours Affectionately,

Swami Yogananda

Kansas City, Missouri
Feb. 20

Dear Doc,

You are a friend in need. Positively plan to come in July or August. Read East–West.* I am opening a summer school. Most leaders from the Centers coming—great teachings. Try utmost to come—good Hindu cooking, great meditations. You remain as my guest—you and Mil. Bring Brad and Bren if convenient.

After March 6th I will be in Los Angeles for one month. Then I go to Louisville, Kentucky.

Please thank Mr. ___. God will save him if he meditates and co-operates. I appreciated his letter.

With deepest blessings—I can not tell you what catastrophe passed thru God's help and what miracle happened since I talked with you on the phone.

Deepest blessings to you all.

Very Sincerely Yours,

S. Yogananda

East–West was the original name of Self-Realization Magazine. In another letter (undated) Paramahansa Yogananda wrote, "I have been working my fingers writing for the tremendous materials in the East–West. I am so happy to be able to express Babaji's, Lahiri Mahasaya's and Guru's teaching. Great truths are coming. Read East–West carefully, and tell all Yogoda is expanding consciousness of man so that it can hold the Christ Consciousness which Jesus had."

The West Hotel
Minneapolis, Minn.
1930

Dear Doc,

Having a great time here. You have done or said nothing —faintly I remember that perhaps you sorrowed with Mrs. Butler that I did not think much of her. Somebody told her I didn't think much of her—please disillusion her I often receive her vibration and like to read her letters. Tell her not to ever doubt this. And tell her to forgive me for not writing for I have hardly time to think of my name. But tell her I love to receive letters for I always do send spiritual replies. I can not tell you about what I don't remember.

Keep up your diet. Don't eat too hot food—just warm. Tell Mildred and children to do same. Too hot food expands cells and is dangerous.

Sometimes at a certain stage of spiritual development the mind becomes negative and speech harsh—it is better to control that and manifest peace, sweet speech and love outwardly and inwardly to all. Please manifest that.

With boundless blessings and love for an awakened Christmas and New Year for you and Mil and Brad and Bren.

With boundless love and blessings,
Very Sincerely Yours,

Swami Yogananda

Mt. Washington Estates
January 20, 1930

Dear Doctor,

I am so happy to have your letters. I have been extremely busy and was away from Mt. Washington after Christmas, otherwise, I should have written you earlier.

Commencing with February everything looks for an upward trend, but, of course, the best is preferred.

Keep on with the prescribed diet for sometime. It will require some time more for you to see me in your meditation—look into the light very steadily. Anyway I am little compared to the Spirit whom you see often in the eye.

Your poem and Christmas message is wonderful and made me very happy.*

With my deepest love and
blessings,

Swami Yogananda

---

*See 1933 East-West Magazine.

San Carlos Hotel
Phoenix, Arizona
Feb. 7, 1930

Dr. M. W. Lewis

Dear One,

When I had no one to turn to I turned to God and He pointed you to me—so has God manifested thru you in the hour of need. If words can convey my love for you do feel what I feel for you. It is wonderful to know that God responds thru His devotees as Himself. Surely in your voice I heard His echo distinctly for the first time. In your laugh I heard His laughter.

I have gone many times to you. This time you must come to me. I was overjoyed to hear of your health. In pursuit of truth which I intuitively feel about anything I fearlessly do—so have I followed my intuitions about the strange methods which I suggested about your health. It needed drastic attention and action.

What I feel about our friendship I spontaneously write.

> God, I care not for riches
> Nor for fame or pomp;
> But give me true friends!
> Even just one, if it be he
> Thru whom I may behold Thee
> And whom I may trust and enjoy without,
> As Thine image,
> E'er reflected in the mirror of my love.
> A friend is he who feels my direst needs as his own,
> Who feels for me as he would feel for himself.

Ah, wavelets of true friendship, heaven-born,
Merge in Thy one ocean of vast Love!
In the sea of friendship
The meandering lost and prodigal souls
Come back to their own one home.

In a hurry thinking of the phone I forgot to talk to Mildred and about Brad and Bren. Please ask Mil to write to me.

Are you coming in July or August?

With boundless love,
Very Sincerely yours,

Swami Yogananda

Mt. Washington Estates
Los Angeles, California
February 11, 1930

Dear Doctor,

I am grieved to know of your ill health. I know exactly what it is—for two weeks stop the exercises then start with twelve in the morning and twelve in the noontime. Keep mind diverted. Don't think of this dull sad pain. I know some others had it. The body has to be tuned in along with the advance of the soul. Your soul has progressed quicker than the body so it is giving trouble. Don't feel discouraged for stopping exercise.

Besides you need absolutely a little rest and traveling. You must come to California and stay with me for one or two months. You will have hill atmosphere plus seashore. I am preparing a place for you all—don't forget that—a place for everlasting happiness.

I am glad you like the *Whispers**—it is finding universal response. Try to explain—after feeling the prayers as per instruction, the meaning will come to you.

With love unceasing to you and blessings to Mil and love to Brad and Bren.

Very Sincerely yours,

Swami Yogananda

Thank you immeasurably for saving institution from jaws of instantaneous death. S.Y.

---

* *Whispers From Eternity* by Swami Yogananda.

Hotel Missouri
St. Louis, Missouri
October 11th

Dear Doctor,

It was awfully sweet of you to call me at Los Angeles. I received your vibrations of joy—I missed you by a little while. I am so happy to know you had been better. Please let me know how you are. I wish I could be with you this minute in body. It is again getting very long and I am impatient to see you all. Your memory and the memory of your family are an everlasting fragrance in my mind. ...

Residential students, harmonious groups staying and making the institution paying. We have extensive vegetable gardens. Wish you were here to drive us in the house-car and be with me and the Infinite by the shore. I am nearing Him in every way. God bless you dear one—forgive delays—you know I write to you a hundred times with my love and my mind. We have thousand pleasant memories unfading, ever-blossoming, pleasant experiences in our mind. Do write to me sooner than I did.

Love and blessings to Brad, Bren, Mil and you,

Swami Yogananda

Los Angeles, California
December 20, 1930

Dear Doc,

Dreadfully sorry for your plight. I am praying deeply for you. You know what causes your trouble is your occasional spiritual doubts and inharmonies in family. Your meditation goes deep but certain little doubts about finances, family etc. cause a clash. Your spiritual horse draws the chariot of your life up but your doubt tries to bring it down. This sets in wrong vibrations which counteracts your spiritual vibrations unbalancing your life force and nervous system which gives birth to diseases.
 Free your mind to be broad and big-hearted as you really are.
 O how I shall miss you all this Christmas. Christmas brings you all nearer than ever.
 Depression is doing its worst than ever. After effects are worse. Next year might begin slightly better times. Let us hope so.
 Sure things which had good probability did not happen. Satan put monkey wrench and my financial state is worse than ever. I have been deeply thinking of my responsibility about the loan. When is that due? Can it be extended for one year more? I am willing to pay—I am not dodging my duty but I am trying to prepare as to what I can do. Please write me a best solution about it. I have a hundred other obligations to meet.
 My Christmas present to you all would be something spiritual and will reach a little after Christmas but my love will reach you, Mildred, Brad and Bren before.
 My new Christmas Card is a novelty. A combination of Cross and Spinal plexuses.
 I shall appreciate if you had gall stones they would have

shown in X-ray. Take another X-ray picture to find if there are any stones. I am deeply praying for you and let me know twice a week how you are.

Give my Christmas and New Years love and greetings to yourself, Mil, Brad, Bren, Roscoe and Dolly. How is Mr. Pierce? Don't think of the disease and bring it back. Forget it.

With deepest love to you.

Very Sincerely yours,

Swami Yogananda

Albany Hotel
Denver, Colorado
July 11, 1931

Dear Doctor,

I received your lovely letter in Milwaukee. I have recently dreadfully missed you and wanted to see you all. Some new happy changes are coming in my life. I am more than ever with God. I have entirely lost consciousness of defeats and victories for God told me in Phoenix when I asked I wanted freedom from everything. He said, "You are already free but think you are not because you looked for freedom in the future. Whether dance of death or dance of life come at your doors—know they come from me and as such rejoice." Ever since I ceased to expect anything.

In Milwaukee I got only three days walk—and I said to the students at the station, "I came singing and dreaming God. I sang, dreamt and felt God with you and in His Songs and Dreams I depart and in His Songs and Dreams we will meet again never to part."

Now, a very devoted student is under my constant care and another student needs the bangle badly. Please do promptly send one immediately and send the other soon—it is a very, very bad case and the bangle will stimulate matters. ...

I will be here till August 12th. Thence I will go to Los Angeles. With deepest love and blessings to you, Mil, Brad and Bren.

With deepest love, Yours,

Swami Yogananda

Los Angeles, California
December 1, 1931

Dear Doctor Lewis,

I was very happy to receive your letter of appreciation. When I hear that other people find in the lessons the beauty and strength they are seeking, it makes me very happy.*

When the sincere desire is there, realization shall come. My only desire is that more people may be awakened through our teachings. I would like them all to have more of beauty and joy in their lives. ...

Wish you were to enjoy Christmas here on the 25th of December. O I so much wish that!

Much love and blessings to you, the children and Mil.

Very sincerely yours,

Swami Yogananda

Dear Mildred,

I deeply thank you for the pictures—I look over them again and again. Wish you were here.

SY

---

*In a letter before 1945, Paramahansaji wrote, "I am glad you like the Precepta — they are the best in America and what India has to offer for they come straight from God. If you see exceptionally good student, give him Kriya — I permit you do so. We must train real people."

Mt. Washington Estates
Los Angeles, California
February 28, 1934

Dear Doctor,

Thank you for your letter which came to hand this morning.

I have already answered Miss ___ letter and sent it airmail. Sorry I could not answer sooner but it seems there are a million things for me to do each day the moment my morning meditation is over.

If you mean the movies we took in Chicago, yes, they have been developed but I haven't yet had the time to see them. This may give you an idea of how busy I am kept. I sent you the other pictures. Please let me know if you wanted the movies.*

I am glad you liked the February pamphlet. Everything is in your control the minute you are convinced of it.

I am enjoying some of the best perceptions of life working in the garden with God-drenched nature all around me and His Presence trembling in my hands.

Please encourage study of Inner Culture East-West Magazine to every student and every seeker you meet. That is highest duty.

With deepest love, I remain,

Very sincerely yours,

S. Yogananda

---

*Dr. Lewis and a fellow disciple met Swami Yogananda in Chicago to attend the 1933 World's Fair.

Los Angeles, California
January 4, 1935

Dear Doc,

Thank you and Mildred for the shirts. They are the most delightful and useful things which you could give unto me. Oh no words can tell you how I missed you at Christmas. The day before Christmas we meditated all day long—God was floating and flooding the garden, the rooms and everything. Everything was fire. You would have seen it as many present beheld the glory of the Infinite.

Best way is to pay up as much life insurance you can. Houses can always be rented but a permanent income is a great thing. ...

Tears came in my eyes when you offered to help. Think but for your help and our Mr. Lynn's help where would we be today. Think what pillars you are of this great work. We have a second temple in town through Mr. Lynn's help. But I never ask him for more than is necessary.

And last work if I can do while my Guruji in India is living. He may be leaving this world anytime—only staying for me and a few. I have great wish to buy a home for this work in India. That would please my Master, your great Guru, most. If you could get $2000 and donate for the temple, then I could ask from Mr. Lynn a few thousand and some more from others and build this temple or buy one already built. It is a shame we have nothing in Calcutta.

So please as you started me in America first, be the first to start for the temple in India. I know unless you give the start, it would be impossible to do anything. Please see that Mildred instead of opposing be also a pillar in this temple in India that would please Babaji, Lahiri Mahasaya and Guru. I know you won't fail me. You will never regret for all you do for God and the Gurus.

I like to announce in Inner Culture Magazine about this India Fund. It is time after 14 years giving my all we do something to establish Gurus' work at Calcutta. Please don't fail me. ...

Please advise me immediately about Bradford and positively tell him I will write.

I was very glad to receive the book of pictures.

You will continue to be well.

With Love Eternal—Yours,

Swami Yogananda

PS   You must come next summer all of you here—drive.

SY

Mt. Washington Estates
Los Angeles, California
March 8 before 1935

Dear Doctor,

Did you receive my joint letter airmailed to you and Mildred? I received your letter dated February 18th. So sorry you have been unwell.

How are ___ and ___ getting along? Recognize you have acquired great powers by these years of meditation, only you must learn to use them to change souls. Don't suffer from inferiority complex—but go forward and change souls. Lahiri Mahasaya will work through you. You should make a great devotee out of ___. He is the one who is guilty in not responding after being saved from losing mind. Please see him often, meditate with him—he will change.

Dear Doctor and Mildred — something more important than India has developed—please give it utmost consideration. This is my supreme request in behalf of the work and never fail me as you never have and proved true children of Lahiri Mahasaya in the hour of need.

Boundless love encircle you and protect you and Mildred ever and ever. I wished you knew what I think of you both—and to whom shall I go for God and Gurus' work but those who have helped me bear my cross and stood with me in times of utter trials. So please forsake me not in my efforts to stabilize this work. God's blessings shall be demonstrated at every turn if you once more respond to my call for His work. Please do realize.

Dear Mildred — always I have been a helper and a guardian of you and your family—so please instead of interrupting please co-operate in Guru's cause and God will co-operate with you.

>With boundless blessings,
>Ever Yours,
>
>S. Yogananda

Los Angeles, California
April 16, 1935

Dear Doctor,

So happy to receive your decision by wire. Blessed be you. Please don't take it wrong—I never scold you—those that are our own them we rebuke for we are interested in their highest good. Everything seems to be going on well.

With unceasing blessings and love,

Very sincerely yours,

Swami Yogananda

Mt. Washington Estates
Los Angeles, California
April 25, 1935

Dear Doctor,

...God and the Masters can do anything by miracle. But then we are left out—so we have to do our best in this Cosmic play and since God is playing and wants us to play hard and when we do our best He is well pleased and then He frees us all to live in His Kingdom evermore.

With unending and blessings to you, Mildred, Brad and Bren, I remain

Very Sincerely Yours,

Swami Yogananda

The National Hotel
Upper Bedford Place
Russell Square
London, W.C.I.
July 2, 1935

Dear Doc and Mil,

Here we are detained for a week lecturing. Enclosed leaflet will speak. Brad is physically well. We have had a nice seeing of sceneries. This meeting has done great things for the message. Introduced to me one of the richest Maharaja of Barode. Invited us to his palace in India. What thanks shall I give for all you have done but my heart's love. I am heart-sick you are not here. What's the use of telling.
   I am so driving constantly I won't try to write much. We are omitting Istanbul. Address up to August 16th, c/o Port Said, Egypt., American Express Co. Reaching Bombay August 22nd then leaving for Calcutta. Always write c/o American Express Co., Calcutta, India.

Expenses are terrific—however getting along through God's Grace.

My eternal love and blessings to you, Mil and Brenda.

With deepest blessings,
Ever yours,

S. Yogananda

July 21

Dear Doctor,

...Please dear Doctor you have been my greatest friend in need next to God, Master and my earthly father.* Someday you all will know how much I have suffered for you all. Please tell Mildred to write me a nice letter. Give her my blessings and love to children and you. I guess Mildred will be fighting to go with me to Heaven.

Yours very sincerely,

Swami Yogananda

Most happy that organization is being looked after ably by you.

SY

---

*In another undated letter, Paramahansaji wrote to Doctor, "Your last help which I was very reluctant to accept came very very handy at this hour. What can I say that would express my love and admiration for your sweet loving unselfish conducts. That is the grandest in American character. God bless that America."

Calcutta
c/o American Express Co.
October 3, 1935

Dear Doctor,

...About getting visions they are never even given to saints on demand and with a discouraged heart. It lies with God alone to grant. This is no excuse—but the truth. No one can bend God. If God would so easily grant visions to create faith in people—there would be no work and people would make their own effort to find Him. One has to move on thorny paths of doubts and bleed profusely and fall many times and untiringly get up in humility and march on before one gets God's vision.

I am enjoying the company of many saints and dozens of young men who are lying prostrate around seeking God through Guru devotion. I am happy that I have to coax none here—I wish you were here—then you would understand.

I am sending to you and Mildred a piece of Swami Sri Yukteswar Giriji's cloth.

Slow and steady wins the race!

Love ever,

S. Yogananda

c/o American Express
Company
Calcutta, India
July 1, 1936

Dear Doc and Mil,

Ever since Master went—I have not felt same. Only the other day I saw him resurrected in a strange new way—and I was very happy. He answered all my questions—I can describe this grand event only when I see you. It surpasses all description. He told me, "Sixteen years I waited for thee but no more—I love thee—I will ever be with thee." He has fulfilled his promise. O I am so happy now. ...

Ever Yours,
Love and blessings to you,

S. Yogananda

[No Date]

Dear Doctor and Mildred,

I am so glad to receive your much expected letter. Please know this for certain Christmas would not be Christmas without you both. St. Lynn's coming is uncertain too. You must come—it pleases the Divine to see you here.

I am glad the agents of the evil-force are ashamed—they should be ashamed after God has worked through you so much from the beginning to help the cause.

Please positively come without fail, come as soon as you can—on the 24th (to meditate) and stay up to January 8th. What is life after all—here it is and then it is gone. Why shouldn't you have this joy with me in the last days—they are rare. I feel God's joy nearest when you are both here.

Keep everything strictly organized in your absence.

Suffering is a part of doing good, parents suffer for children, Christ suffered for all. You suffered last time and now you know. Conquer all with love—give love anyway even Satan turns some against you.

Come you must. With deepest love to you, Mil, Brad and Bren.

S. Yogananda

Everybody is expecting you—your presents are already here.

S. Y.

Golden Lotus Temple
October 31 — no year

Dear Doc and Mil,

Long have you gone and how much I miss you both. So you must come this Christmas. You both will have the cutest and newest likable Christmas present that you ever had. I have got them already—so you must come and stay as long as you can.

At last the Ganges property is ours—through the sacrifice and Divine co-operation of both of you. What you have done will remain with you forever. ...

God's good children should suffer together for God's work and should not forsake one another at the time of utmost need. Heaven will never forsake you, if you forsake not Heaven in the hour of its need.* Heaven and Truth are constantly struggling against the forces of Maya to re-establish themselves.

Everybody likes to ride in the decorated gilded car—few help to make it. Our hands are about to finish the Yogoda car for posterity to ride it—why not let us all put our hands together and finish it.

I want you to know it is my responsibility to the great work, you and a few others for which I am trying to financially save the work instead of freeing myself from this constant heavy burden on my soul for the responsibility of others' life. Please understand distinctly that my prosperity will mean your prosperity, my financial freedom your freedom.

---

*Several years later (1944), Paramahansaji wrote, "We must suffer and worry and work and plan for God — then He will do the same for us."

If ever a friend I loved—I loved you and love—so nothing shall please me than to see you free. Why do you doubt?

With deepest love,

Swami Yogananda

Mt. Washington Estates
Los Angeles, California
March 22, 1938

Dr. M. W. Lewis
29 Edgehill Road
Arlington, Mass.

Dear Doctor,

Many thanks for your letter of March 18 which was awaiting me upon my return from Encinitas. I have been mostly living at Los Angeles due to pressure of work. I am extremely delighted you got rid of the house. Now try to sell the other house for ??? or better. Moving into an apartment is fine. It is so less expensive.
    Glad old ___ is one of the old faithful. Give him my love. I often think of him. Tell him all he is doing I am cognizant of it in spirit. He will win greatly in the end. It is the spirit which counts.
    It would be a good idea the way you plan to come to Los Angeles. Lots of papayas and sunshine and our love. It is alright for Mil and Bren and her friend to come by car and how long can you stay?

With deepest love and blessings to you, Mil and children,

Yours sincerely,

S. Y.

Self-Realization Fellowship
Los Angeles, California
May 27, 1938

Dear Mildred,

I was glad to receive your letter but have been going back and forth and was unable to reply earlier.

As for your staying here and working for your board, if you promise to make a good chana curry once in a while that is the best thing I could ask of you.

In your letter you have presented me with so many complex problems that I don't know what to say. I am sure the jobs are not available in California except to Californians and don't know if Brenda could get work here for the summer. I believe there is a law requiring one to live here for some months before work can be obtained. In other words, Californians come first in California. Your letter is not clear and so I cannot say anything about ___ but I am glad that she has realized what it would mean to get into an orthodox family after being trained in liberal beliefs.

If you feel you can't come now, could you and Doctor and Brenda all come together in August and stay for a month? Whatever you decide is all right with me. Please use your reason in the situation you are in and let me know immediately what you are planning to do, because it is for you to know best the circumstances you are in—but whatever you decide will be all right with me.

Desire should not be thwarted. However, college life will settle her career. In the meantime if she comes here and talks things over—then we can settle matters and she would have a glimpse of this life here and compare with her own present life. Then she can decide.

So try again to come in June. Happiness is more than money. Money is a slave of those who pursue true happiness.

Unceasingly pray and meditate. Make every minute an altar of God. Thank you unceasingly. Everyone misses you very much. "Guru—Dr. Lewis and Mil" I extremely miss you and whenever I can I will be with you. Please try to be bigger as you are and bring back ___ the fold. He needs guidance. Give them my blessings.

       Very Sincerely Yours,

       Swami Yogananda

c/o New House Hotel
Salt Lake City, Utah
July, 1938

Dear Doc,

At last I heard from Mildred—she is passing through here. I hope she sees me. I got a letter that she, Brenda and a friend already started and you are not coming. I am heart-broken. You must come—you must come—you must come—you must come—you must come—and pass your August vacation as early as possible. No getting away from it.

Let me know how Brad is and the dear Yogoda folks. I am giving a campaign here until 12th of July. Then back to Encinitas for August—you must come. Please write me here by airmail that you are coming.

Ever yours,

S. Yogananda

Encinitas, California
September 22, 1938

Dear Doctor,

Your most loving letter received. I am overjoyed to see you noticed the change in Mildred. I had prayed for her too—and with her effort—she is so changed. That's what I wanted always her to be to you. I am glad beyond dreams.

You are in God's and the Great Ones' hands—there is nothing to fear. Have infinite reliance.

Words fail to describe how joyous I feel for your joy and for the cause and for ___ for the victory over her soul. She is one of the loveliest souls you can imagine—sweet like a fragrant flower. Whenever she resisted my efforts she was with darkness and hated me—but now being in light she listens even to my whispers. You can well imagine how happy I am.

Things are happening fast for the work and it shall please me most to see you all here and in India all fixed when I go. I came with nothing and will take nothing from India or America when I go—only I came with God and with Him I will go and wait for you all to welcome there where there will be no condition to our happiness or existence.

God is most wonderful. He loves us so silently and wonderfully and thru the devotees.

I am so happy for your great help to the work—some great good will come out of it. I will inform you as soon as final arrangements are started.

With boundless blessings to you and Mildred—for your soul cooperation in being instruments of the Divine for the furtherance of the work in a most important moment.

With my unending love, I
remain ever yours,

Yogananda

Give my deepest love to yourself and Mildred—am ever pleased for your and especially her willingness to cooperate.

P.S.

You will never know what joy it was to see ___ changed. Do you know I knew Satan was turning her against me and the work—and you knew I knew my words were futile—so I asked the Father, Divine Mother and the Gurus—and silently kept on telling them in the car. And the miracle of the Lord happened. Satan was driven away from her and God pulled her in the work. ... ___ had responded once to me and thru that the Divine Grace worked. And that was wonderful to see our loved child change. There is no greater joy that to see our loved ones protected in God. Mildred I am so happy for you.

God has fulfilled one of my greatest prayers, for I always wanted to do something to please you most as you always have pleased me in my tribulations.

S.Y.

Mt. Washington Estates
Los Angeles, California
October 12, 1938

Dear Mildred,

Thank you for your dear letter. I have been busy beyond words. Book and new project, God and a million things have attracted my entire time.

I am so happy beyond dreams that you and Doctor are so great friends and friends with me. I shall never call you Mildred for I never imagined how steadily and continuously you have really milled all my dreads about your temper forever and become a saintly lady. This is not flattery but from my very heart. And we three are beyond measure happy that turned back the tide of her life from matter to God of her own accord.

We expect with God guiding us to have a wonderful place of all religions.

Anyway, be sure you and Doctor are coming for Christmas and must stay until January 8th when the second anniversary of the Encinitas Temple will be held.

Your co-operation with me in the kitchen was most efficient and extremely enjoyed.

With my unending love and blessings to Doctor and you, mildest Mildred, I remain,

                              Ever Sincerely Yours,

                              Yogananda

Los Angeles, California
February 2, 1939

Dear Doc,

I am glad to receive your letter. You will never know how I miss you. There is something—some bond from the past between you and me which gives indescribable joy when we are together in God and it pains me when you are gone. ...

Parents are the instruments of God and they help the help-less baby to grow up—so the baby when it grows up with the life-blood of parents, he or she might follow the parents' wishes for his or her benefit.

I received a nice letter from Bradford and Mildred. I am replying to them in enclosed.

I am doing big things everything succeeding. I won't delay one day more than that day the Divine tells you to come bag and baggage. There is plenty of work.

Could you without much complication keep the funds ready in case I need it. If I don't I won't but something big is pending so I write as I know you won't fail. You have been my right hand and Divine instrument from the beginning—continue being so and you will reach the end. Awfully glad Boston Center is improving—keep on—so that it becomes a hive with lots of Divine honey. Boston is my first God-hive in this country—that's why it is so dear to me.

Ever yours,

Yogananda

Love to the group.

Los Angeles, California
June 27, 1939

Dr. M. W. Lewis
29 Edgehill Road
Arlington, Mass.

Dear Doc and Mil,

Your letter greatly delighted me. I wondered what delayed the reply and I was going to write the night before your letter arrived—when something told me to wait and lo in the morning your letter came. ...

A childhood dream and all because mostly for your instrumentality and God and the Great Ones. My heart is full what shall I say.

Summer sun is wonderful—come home running both of you. I am extremely glad ___ is doing well and joining Boston Center regularly. Practice Kriya with him—that alone might give him new vision.

With undying love to you both and personally grateful that you have been such noble instruments of God.

Ever yours,

Yogananda

Immediately write approximate date of your arrival. Your coming is my thrill of summer.

PY

Mt. Washington Estates
Los Angeles, California
January 20, 1940

Dear Doctor,

I was glad to get your letter and to know of your arrival home. I miss you and Mildred and hope the time will come when you won't have to leave here. Let us pray for that. I appreciate your beautiful spirit. You will always have my blessings and good will that you may reach your highest goal. When friendship is founded in Spirit it never dies. ...

Please keep me informed as to how things are with you all. Give Mildred my love and blessings and tell her to meditate deeply whenever she can.

With unceasing blessings and love,

Very sincerely yours,

Paramhansa Yogananda

P. S.

It has been quite lonesome since you left. So far I am planning a motor trip from Loredo by the New Highway to Mexico City. It is only 700 miles from Loredo to Mexico City. You both can meet me there coming by train. Can you come there by May 1st or June 1st or July 1st—if I decide to go there. I would like to go only when mangoes are ripe. I am getting ready. You can return from Loredo to Boston or via Los Angeles as you wish. Please let me know at once. I am saving up for this trip. I know you are going to enjoy. If it is to be a railroad trip, I will let you know.

With boundless love and blessings to you and Mildred, I remain,

                    Very sincerely yours,

                        P. Yogananda

Los Angeles, California
May 15, 1940

Dear Doctor,

I have just received your last letter written May 5th. So at last you are settled in your apartment. I hope that Mildred is all right again after so much activity.

What are Bradford and Brenda doing?

Most people are seeking new things all the time. They are too restless and thoughtless to want to settle down to any particular study. And they don't want to make the effort, either physically, mentally or spiritually in order to get out of their troubles.

The best thing to do is to keep on trying to the best of your ability. Those few souls who are sincere will be attracted to our work sooner or later.

If we don't go to Mexico—you are positively coming here in August for a full month or more. I am planning vacation with yours. I must have vacation. I will let you know soon—but be prepared to come here on seven days notice.

Give Mildred my blessings and my love to you both.

Blessings,

P. Yogananda

Golden Lotus Temple
Encinitas, California
June 25, 1940

Dear Doc and Mildred,

To the last minute I tried to go to Mexico but war conditions, red tape, political situation, Immigration declare it unsafe for me to go there. So to avoid tragedy out of a pleasure trip I have given up the idea. But you must come, reach here by August 5th and stay up to September 5th or come by August 1 and leave on September 1. I might have to go on a lecture tour September 7th, so please come accordingly. I have lots of plans for nice short trips when you come—go to San Francisco again or visit the redwoods or Yosemite whatever you like. I have gotten a new boat at Lake Hodges for your coming. We all are looking forward to you coming. Don't disappoint by delay.

Please write at once your exact day of arrival that we can make our plans definitely from now on. Write by airmail as I must have time to prepare. How are Brad and Bren and you both?

Give my love to yourself and Mildred and all the group and Sister Yogamata.

With deepest love and joy of waiting for your arrival.

Very sincerely yours,

P. Yogananda

P.S. It is very sad—Paramananda passed.

Mt. Washington Estates
Los Angeles, California
Sept. 18, 1940

Dear Doc and Mil,

Thank you for your letters with their beautiful spirit which I have just received. ...I miss you and Mildred very much but am comforted that you will be returning in a few months.

Glad Roscoe and Dolly liked the dish. Please give them both my good wishes and blessings. ...

Your letters are deeply touching. You must know how I miss you both when you are gone. You are my oldest dears in America. Do remember me to dear Sister Yogamata.

With unending blessings,

Very Sincerely Yours,

Swami Yogananda

Mt. Washington Estates
Los Angeles, California
June 2, 1941

Dr. M. W. Lewis

Dear Doctor,

I have received your letter of May 12 and am glad you are making some effort. When do you expect to come here this year? As always, I am looking forward to that time. How is Mildred? She hasn't written to me for a long time. Please let me know at once when you will arrive. The swimming pool is waiting for you. ...

I can't wait until you come. It is only when you work, slave, borrow, go through all kinds of difficulties for God's work and Him as we do for our earthly families—then God is pleased. Then He knows we love the Giver more than His gifts.

Why do I keep myself poor—forgetting my own personal security, because I love Him and want to do His will to the last no matter what it costs me. Nothing is accomplished without supreme effort.

Now I am waiting—it seems the time is fast approaching when I will see your smiling faces. Only I dread the time when you leave. How is Bradford and his wife and Brenda? Give them all my love and blessings. Very deepest love and unceasing blessings to you and Mildred.

Very sincerely yours,

P. Yogananda

Los Angeles, California
June 17, 1941

Dear Doctor,

As time is approaching I am anxiously waiting for your arrival. Come home joyously. I am planning a different but very joyous vacation together. You will enjoy I know.

With unceasing blessings to you and Mildred, I remain,

Very sincerely yours,

P. Yogananda

P.S. Believe in Him and work thru Him and His grace will flow through you.

P.Y.

Washington D. C.
September 24, 1941

Dr. and Mrs. Lewis

Dear Ones,

At last after many wonderful times—I am headed towards Boston via Philadelphia and New York. I will finish Philadelphia and New York by Tuesday. Expecting to reach Boston Wednesday. Please arrange a full meeting (by letting everyone know by telephone etc.) on Thursday 8:00 P.M. at Boylston Street. Please ask ___ to announce next Sunday of my coming. I will lecture on "Who was Jesus Before."

I will stay in Boston one week and would like to go to Duxbury on the weekend with you and Mildred. Then upon our return, we can invite a few for a special dinner one night at your home and view some motion picture films of Mt. Washington and Encinitas.

I will wire you the time of my arrival and Mildred can meet me at the station if it conflicts with your office time.

Deepest love to you both,

P. Yogananda

Mt. Washington Estates
Los Angeles, California
November 12, 1941

Dr. and Mrs. M. W. Lewis
Boston, Massachusetts

Dear Doctor and Mildred,

Both of your deeply touching letters reached me in Washington. I am happy beyond dreams that Mildred is like her former self.

I am so sorry I didn't see more of you, Doctor, during my visit in Boston but I surely was glad that Mildred could go with me. It was sweet of you both to give me such a nice apartment for it was my ambition during my early days in Boston, to live in an apartment but I was not able to afford one. Really, you both fulfilled that long-felt desire. In this you were an instrument of God, no doubt.

I am waiting to see you both. Without fail or without any doubt you must come here at Christmas and stay up to the tenth of January, and get rested up for I see that you so violently work without cessation while you are in Boston. This is your only chance to rest. I am looking forward to having some vacation when you come.

With deepest, boundless blessings to you and Mildred, I am,

Very sincerely yours,

Paramhansa Yogananda

P.S. Undying love to both of you. Come home soon—try to attend meditation if possible. Deepest love again. I am impatient to be with you. This is the truth of my heart.

P. Y.

Los Angeles, California
November 26, 1941

Dear Doctor,

I was happy to receive your letter. But the most unhappy note was when you wrote you can't come.

There will be no Christmas unless you come. Already I have so many presents for you, you must come to get them.

Please airmail your reply at once without delay by what train you are coming. Come on December 23 and stay until 7th of January.

God will keep you and Mildred well. Enjoy your trip. We will be waiting.

My deepest love and blessings to you.

Very sincerely yours,

P. Yogananda

Mt. Washington Estates

1942

To Doctor and Mildred,

I know your spiritual influences worked and it was indescribably nice for ___ to help in a great moment of need. I have written to him. He is certainly a camouflaged spiritual diamond. He has rough exterior but has surprising good inside.

It was awfully sweet of you to say and ask as to my opinion as to what you want to give. Thus I became tongue-tied—you have done so much—do give what you can without discomforting yourself. I certainly need help. I have gone agriculturing with a tractor. Thanks a million for help through ___ and for sending more.

I can't wait until you both come and we will have good times together. Meditate unceasingly.

With deepest love,
Very sincerely yours,

P. Yogananda

Mt. Washington Estates
Los Angeles, California
1942

Dear Mildred and Doc,

I was the recipient of your letter but I did not enjoy the tone in it as to the uncertainty of your coming. I specially arranged for the opening of the temple (if it is finished and can be finished) on August 30th. You must stay until September 7th. Enjoy the Divine surrounding while you can—never can tell what comes next. I have been taking special interest to build this temple with extreme beauty and thought—as you both are the real founders of the temple. Remember your donation at last has borne fruit in two super-institutions (one by the Ganges) and another in the heart of Hollywood from which our work will spread all over.

God expects me to do my very best and finish the "Hollywood SRF Church of All Religions." You must come—life is too short to neglect the little while of pure joy which we receive in mutual company. Really when you see it then you will say it is going to be one of the most beautiful churches in Hollywood. At least I think so.

With unceasing blessings,

Swami Yogananda

Los Angeles, California
[1942 ?]

Dear Doc and Mildred,

Here the Lord kept me continuously from going to bed and I was feeling a mental discomfort when your telephone calls came.*

I was very glad to hear your voices both of you, Doctor and Mildred. So sorry you had to go through this intense agony and test.

In spite of all curative suggestions remember God and the Great Ones are your supreme anchor and you must remember—a very strong change of mind during the stubborn mentality of pain and sickness, is the best and supreme antidote. So be anchored in God while doing reasonable things for undoing the unconsciously perpetrated past karmas. Exercise whenever able.

Received your telegram, glad you Doctor are more comfortable. I went through your suffering—but be brave and conquer. God is with you. I am glad the Doctor verified what I saw within.

Practice all said over the telephone as you feel they respond. Write me every day by airmail how you are getting along. Mentally pray all the time, "Father, manifest Thy perfection through my body." Fear nothing—you will be completely well through the Grace of God, Gurus and your faith.

---

*Dr. Lewis referred to this letter as "Changing the Cosmic Picture." He said, "In case of karmic disturbances in Boston of such severity I called the Master in California."

My deepest love and sympathy to you, Mildred and Brad and Bren.

>Very Sincerely yours,
>
>Paramhansa Yogananda

Los Angeles, California
January 10, 1942

Dear Doctor,

I was glad to receive your letter. But you know that I definitely told you, you must come. No amount of money could induce me to forego the pleasure of seeing you both—you know that.*

So please never give me any alternative when it concerns your coming. Why I have been breaking my neck to fix the temple that you may rejoice to see it. It will take away most of my pleasure if you don't come. Then I won't have any excuse for vacation. We have been getting ready for your coming. Money or no money—it is unthinkable that you won't come. So please positively buy your tickets now and arrive on the 7th of August and stay till 7th or 8th of September. Life is too short to forego the joy of seeing you both.

With deepest love and blessings to you both.

Sincerely yours,

P. Yogananda

---

*On one occasion after Doctor and Mrs. Lewis visited with the Master, he wrote them, "The Lord granted my prayer and wish that you come on your vacation in gladness and without worries. Yes God does everything—if we come to know His ways and learn to love Him. He is our nearest of the near and the dearest of the dear."

Los Angeles, California
January 21, 1942

Dear Doctor and Mildred,

I address you both, even though Mildred did not write me a line.

This is the honest truth—it took me days to get used to being without you both. I kept seeing Doctor standing before me in the overcoat—with his head tipped backward and reverential.*

And I saw Mildred all blushing with spring youthfulness. This is not putting Mildred ahead of Doctor but a description of what I saw. And I can't wait until the summer comes.

With deepest love and boundless blessings to you and Mildred,

Very sincerely yours,

P. Yogananda

---

*The overcoat had originally belonged to Paramahansaji, and he had later given it to Dr. Lewis.

Los Angeles, California
February 7, 1942

Dear Doctor and Mildred,

I was very happy to receive your letters. I am glad your physical problem is decreasing. There are some small problems still—they will all be dissolved. That's what I am praying.

Don't omit your exercises. This was a part of shakedown to test your consciousness and to show you how terrible the world is. There is little or no happiness here so we should seek it within and with God alone. Imagine those that are being tested on the battlefields with body parts blown away—with shrapnel lodged in their flesh. But God has blessed you with great faith and you need not worry. I am glad you are so faithful in everything you do.

I was so happy to hear from you, Mildred, and glad Doctor has such a friend and helper. Imagine if you were here and Doctor suffering such crucifixion in Massachusetts—what you would have felt.

With my unceasing love and blessings,
Very sincerely yours,

Paramhansa Yogananda

Los Angeles, California
April 21, 1942

Dear Doc and Mildred,

What can I say at your generosity—Roscoe, you and Boston have principally saved my life at this hour. The Hollywood temple is bought waiting for the rains to cease so that it can be shipped to our place in Hollywood. It is the cutest thing you ever saw. It has a stage, blue screen, wonderful electrical fixtures. The more I see it the more I like it. ...

A million thanks for your timely help. You must come in August—it is coming near.

With deepest love and blessings to both of you.

Very sincerely yours,

P. Yogananda

Los Angeles, California
September 29, 1942

Dear Doctor and Mildred,

    I was very glad to receive your letter. I have missed you both very very much. It is needless to tell you how much I want you both here.

    I am happy you could join Grandpa Lewis' ceremony on time. He impressed me much by his visit when I was last there—so I wrote about him in Inner Culture. I really loved Grandpa—because your sweet body (Doctor's) came from him and he was so nice to me. I am very pleased you and all of your relatives liked my poems—they were real heart outbursts. Somehow Grandpa so looked like my father and really I felt for him like I felt for my earthly father. After long I saw father one night just as I saw Grandpa Lewis and I know he is happy for his release. Your words of appreciation and sweet words from your heart are priceless to me. You know what I feel for you both.

All my love to you both,

P. Yogananda

SRF Headquarters
December 25, 1942

To Dr. Lewis

Dear Doctor,

So happy inexpressibly that you are here to receive a few gifts from me.

No words can tell the joy you bring to me personally and to so many here.

This is my spiritual gift to you, "From this Christmas and New Year you redouble your efforts at meditation—now you have to convince the Father that you want Him badly and that you are constantly working in meditation and holy activity to please Him. Remember whatever you do He knows—so don't ever blame Him for delaying to answer with His Complete Presence. When the time will be ripe He will come. Never doubt Him but ever question even your deepest efforts to be with God.

Just plunge in Him and swim in Joy and you will reach His Shores."

With unceasing blessings,
Very sincerely yours,

Paramhansa Yogananda

Mt. Washington Estates
Los Angeles, California
January 13, 1943

Dear Doctor,

...We dreadfully miss you. I could hardly eat—for it did not taste any good after you left. I enjoyed food through you.

Try utmost this time to transfer yourself. Find out the laws. And if God grants you this—you must live in the way I plan for you then alone you will be happy. Remain behind things but not in it.

With unceasing love and blessings to you and Mildred.

Sincerely yours,

P. Yogananda

Los Angeles, California
March 4, 1943

Dear Doc & Mil,

I was glad to receive your letters and must answer combined to save time. Besides you both are two in one—so I may just as well write to the one in two.

God is the first goal of life—first, last and all the time. Quicker you find it out quicker the release from this terrible painful conundrum of contradictions. So little for any mortal to understand when it baffles saints to know a little bit of God's ways. I am not wasting time I have added six hours silence every week—and I find it wonderful. I have added that to my regular exercising which I hope I will never miss. Why don't you try it too.

Deepest love to you both and Brad and Bren.

Ever Yours,

P. Yogananda

Golden Lotus Hermitage
Encinitas, California
June 11, 1943

Dear Doc and Mil,

...Well, I am looking forward to your coming—and this time we will stay here. I never enjoyed Encinitas as now. I was too fussing with everything here and had no time to enjoy, so Lord took Golden Lotus. Now I am free to enjoy here and build more churches. ...

Really I never enjoyed Encinitas as now—I wished I had done this eight years ago—so many books would have been finished. So much time of life is gone. ...

Try to suggest or raise a little for S.R.F. Church in San Diego. I gave all loose cash I could get hold of—still some need. It is almost as beautiful as Hollywood—different and grand. No matter what you raise—always expenses seem to be greater. Ask Roscoe, Dolly whatever they can of free will—I have no desire to touch for my own account. They put their hands in one church—ask them to put in another. I am very happy about their son—good comes—by being in touch with good.

Meditate deeply and unceasingly. Give my welcome to the little one coming in behalf of Brad and wife. Brenda has not written—I have been expecting a letter from her.

With unceasing blessings
and deepest love,

P. Yogananda

P.S. I am impatiently waiting for you — then vacation specifically begins. Deepest love to you both.

Mt. Washington Estates
March 12, 1944

Dear Doc and Mil,

You never can tell the joy which I received on receiving the wire about Bradford. When hundreds of thousands of agonized mothers' offsprings are being wrenched away from their God-pleading bosoms—and when world karma is so strong it is very hard to make the Heavenly Father listen—however, in spite of that I have fervently asked Him as deeply as I can knowing your feelings and my feelings seeing Bradford grow up and so change spiritually and affectionately. All things are possible unto Him and keep steady unswerving faith. Please let me know everything—all turns of events.* ...

I am overjoyed to see you are earnestly going after a centre in Boston—my first love in America. We must do as much good as possible while alive. Everyone lives for self and takes risks for self. We must live for God and take risks for Him.

Sitting by the Charles River with Sister Yogamata, I used to be consumed with the desire and urge for a Boston Center. When a permanent Center is created, the atmosphere would be different and it will grow when advertized and regularly taken care of. There should be a nice altar and spiritual atmosphere. The symptomatic treatment of a permanent Center would give new confidence in people. The corner lot is very attractive but is a problematic thing and will tie up money without accomplishing anything. If a small church with gold dome could be made it would have

---

*On another occasion (undated), Paramahansaji wrote: "Since virtue is so hidden by obvious triumphs of vice — God alone can show how His unbeatable virtue secretly wins in the end. Wars are not won only by big cannons or money but by good national karma and God's Grace."

been wonderfully attractive. ...

This would be the climax of your leaving Boston for good. And it will be a wonderful gesture on your part to give to the Boston Center which you managed so long. I know I told you not to give anymore—so did I think of not spending from the capital or necessary funds—but still I have to do—such is our path.* We should do for God even when we can not—that's what pleases Him. It will stand as a permanent monument of your work and culmination of your work at Boston. Please concentrate.

With unceasing deepest love to you both and Brad and Bren.

Ever yours,

P. Yogananda

---

*In May of 1924, Paramahansaji wrote, "In this momentary dream of life when others are smiling with material dream (success) only to wake up in nightmare of suffering we must dream for God—hold ambition for God's work."

Mt. Washington Estates
May 25, 1944

Dear Doctor and Mildred,

Thanks for your letter. Am glad to know that you don't want to get rid of our little church in Long Beach. But we did receive quite an offer for it—much more than we paid.

About coming, better plan to come here, leaving Boston July 31st, arriving in Los Angeles on August 3rd. Then we will go to Encinitas the 5th for I have my services there on the 6th.

Am doing most important things which you will learn more about when you come.

Deepest love and blessings to you both. Am looking forward to your coming again. Unendingly busy.

Love to all, you Mil, Brad and Bren. It will be very nice to see you.

Paramhansa Yogananda

Encinitas, California
1945

Dear Doc and Mil,

Thanks for your letters dated March 11. ...We are advancing in God but life's time is getting short not longer—that's all I meant. You don't have to know how big God is—all you can do now is to taste Him as the ever new Joy of meditation. Doubts and discouragements don't help. Faith brings us nearer to Him. I am glad you made some resolutions with the New Year.

I am happy you saw the living face of Jesus. Our faith makes God living i. e. manifest. Only He is hidden.

One has to practice deeper and deeper until calmness and joy become a second nature like the habit of the body which is built thru incarnations. Just make joy of meditation ever with you. Never think it is away and it will stay. As you can't forget the body so time will come when you couldn't forget the Joy of the soul.

When devotees sincerely work they sure get Divine Grace. But God never surrenders until He is thoroughly and completely sure of the devotee. That's why it takes so long because He is sitting behind all things.

He will never throw you into oblivion. You will be consciously ushered out of body by Guru.* You have earned it by all these years of Kriya Yoga practice. I don't know yet about Mildred, but your good Karma will help her and I will help her.

The mother gave freedom to the child. The child got drunk and misused freedom and wandered into a marsh.

---

*In another letter (no date), Paramahansaji wrote, "I know not how to thank you in words — many times you have been a great friend in need. You shall ever find me when your Highest Need comes at the end of this drama of life. Keep faith steadily."

The child was sinking but didn't realize the danger to life because he was drunk—so did not wish to get out much and did not know he was sinking due to drunkenness—but his mother suddenly came and wished to save him but could not because her son misused his freedom and got himself beyond her help. In this case the mother was more eager to save the son than the son to save himself. So are we drunk with ignorance—do not realize the depth of our continuous suffering of the future—so Divine Mother cannot free us without using our free will. And if we don't choose to be free—there is none who can free us.

Many thanks for your donation—it helps much for I help India. But you must come on August 7th—no getting away from that. Mildred please get a good medium-sized washing machine with a ringer. Please meditate more that you can catch up for lost time. A good second hand washing machine of a good make ought to be good.

About our conversation of coming here—we talk back and forth each expecting the other to take the initiative. You must take the initiative. (1) please answer if Dr. Lewis is freshening up for his examination in Los Angeles next August. Do you know the exact time the exam will take place? Indeed, coming to California is not as difficult as finding God.

I am awfully glad the Vibrator saved you time and energy. ... I am very happy you got what I wanted you to get for Doctor. They are hard to find. Your will-power, plus to save your own neck (rather than massage him for hours of eternity) you made me very happy.

I am glad Brenda is happy. Both of you please receive my love and blessings. Tell Brad and Bren and Brad's wife I send my love and prayers. What has Brenda decided?

With deepest love and blessings to you and Doc,

                              Paramahansa Yogananda

Mt. Washington Estates
Los Angeles, California
February 8, 1945

Dear Mildred,

Was so happy to get your letter and to know that you both and Sister arrived in Boston safely. I no longer think of Boston as your home now—for you and Doc will be settled in good old sunny California.

We are looking forward to having you both here never to part again by your going back.

I am glad Brenda is coming along fine. Give her my blessings. Things are popping here. Thank Doctor for the bangle. St. Lynn was highly pleased.

Love to Roscoe, Dolly, to you both and Brad and Bren.

Just packing for L. A.

Sincerely yours,

P. Y.

Los Angeles, California
August 3, 1945

Dear Mildred,

Many thanks for your letter. I am happy thinking about your coming here at last. I like the attitude you are taking. Remember the story I have always told about the original plan the Indian savants advised for man to follow. After fulfilling his duties as a householder, raising children and working for them, then man's later years should be spent in meditation and working for God.

I will be praying that everything goes right when you tell your family members about your plans. It isn't as if you were moving to the ends of the earth. Just remain calm within.

My deepest love and blessings to both of you, to Brad and Bren and to your family.

Very sincerely yours,

P. Yogananda

Mt. Washington Estates
Los Angeles, California
September 19, 1945

Dear Doctor and Mil,

Glad to receive your letter and to know that everything is working out harmoniously so that you can come here. Let me know when you will be coming.

Last Sunday Dick Elliott called me at Church when I was giving the Initiation and he came right out and took the Initiation. I had expected him to go to Mt. Washington and stay but he had to return to the base that night. He looks well and seems happy over his good fortune. I was so happy to see Dick intact and well. He is a very fine boy and Navy life hasn't seemed to hurt him at all. I told him that part of his father's gift to the work had enabled us to build the "Church of All Religions" in Hollywood. ...

When are you coming? I am working furiously night and day. It won't be long now!

With love and blessings,

P. Yogananda

Mt. Washington Estates
Los Angeles, California
October 7, 1945

Dear Doctor,

Received your letter and one from Brenda too. Please thank her and tell her I am looking forward to her coming around the same time that you and Mildred leave for Los Angeles and to your coming.*

Am eagerly waiting for your arrival now, when we can make plans together. Come, or rather, plan to leave Boston around the 21st. There should be a better chance to get sufficient gas at that time. I am so happy Bradford took the matter of Boston leadership with the right spirit. A chip off the old spiritually solid blocks (you and Mil) ought to do something in Boston.

Please let me know distinctly when you arrive.

With unceasing love and blessings,

P. Yogananda

---

*Dr. and Mrs. Lewis moved permanently to California in October 1945.

Encinitas, California
March 26, 1946

To Doc Lewis

Dear One of Yore,

> This birthday of yours I celebrate as ne'er before
> Your coming on earth
> Has been to us all and Mildred a source of mirth
> May your life ever be
> A spiritual pattern for others to see
> And follow—to the one abode of light
> Where all must go by living right.

Happy Birthday to you.

Happy Birthday to you.

With boundless blessings to you and Mil-bliss,

Paramhansa Yogananda

A little token from my heart.

PY

Los Angeles, California
April 17, 1949

Dear Doc,

Happy Easter to you Mildred and Bren. Tell Brenda I enjoyed her letter and am happy for her and am praying.

Thanks a million for doing such good work with the Supervisors.*

I like your conservative sincere way of moulding worldly people. I am so happy you succeeded in every undertaking and (ticklish ones too). God bless you for all you are doing and becoming popular in serving people with your fine services because of years of Kriya practice and blessings of Gurus. Do everything to please God and Gurus to the end and you will reach your coveted goal. Give up all mundane desires for the desire for God only.

Please save some good ripe Papayas for me when I go to Encinitas next week.

With my unceasing blessings to the trio,

Very sincerely yours,

P. Yogananda

---

*San Diego County Board of Supervisors.

Los Angeles, California
March 26, 1951

Dr. M. W. Lewis

Dear One,

Your birthday has brought great delight to your friends, family and especially to those of us who spiritually know you and your constant effort to please God, Christ and the Gurus.

May all of us celebrate many of your birthdays. Happy Birthday to you.

With all my love and blessings

Very Sincerely Yours,

S. Yogananda

Encinitas, California
April 26, 1951

Mildred and Dr. Lewis

Dear Ones,

It seems like old times and much more since you both and Brenda so from within work for God. My scolding is love of God for very few care for you in this world except what they can get out of you.

Your invitation "come again soon" seems so sweet—it had a magnet call. Poverty and want are good for it makes us appreciate the richest possession in our true friends. ...

Very Sincerely yours,

Paramhansa Yogananda

Chapter 4
Divine Friendship

> *Hollywood Temple*
> *December 15th, 1959*
>
> *"I am glad you attend Doctor's lectures. He gives not only the words, but the Spirit behind the words."* — Paramahansa Yogananda to a group at one of the SRF services.

This subject is very dear to the hearts of us all. True love is a very difficult subject to speak about because, as Master said, "Divine Love is a celestial experience"—very difficult to put into words. The one Divine Love which is underneath all true friendship is none other than the pull of God—the pull of His great attractive force drawing all things back home to Him. That is the greatest force in the Universe, far greater than the force of creation, for all things dissolve back finally into God.

And so friendship, we must realize, is of God. True friendship is none other than Spirit's attempt to return from duality, from relativity, from multiplicity, back into the unity of the One. God has become many, and He is sitting in the hearts of each one of us. He is trying to return home to Himself. And that's why every true friendship is of God, and every true friendship has the bond of Divine Love, Unconditional Love. So friendship is one of the greatest aspects of God, one of the greatest phases of God's Omnipresence and Omniscience.

Everything *is* in God. Whatever aspect you want to approach Him as—Heavenly Father, Mother, Friend, Beloved—is there. He is the One. And because He is the One, He is trying to return home to that Oneness. Having made creation, that He might express Himself in so many ways, now He wants to go back home to Himself. Friendship is the way. Friendship is perhaps the greatest, quickest path back to God, because when you have the guru-disciple relationship, it is the greatest friendship. That is the spiritual law of returning back home to God.

This pull of God, of course, changes. It is metamorphosed into many forms. Human love, family love is none other than Divine Love, but it is just a little different, because there are conditions and restrictions. Sometimes, in these various forms of love, there is attachment and possession. That dilutes Divine Love. Divine Love is none other than God's unconditional love, His unconditional pull of everybody, irrespective of color, class or creed. There are no conditions to God's love. There are conditions sometimes to human love and friendship, but true friendship has for its matrix, or cementing bond, the Divine Love of God's presence. The greatest example of this Divine Love is the guru-disciple relationship.

True friendship is based on the broadness and unconditional love of God, and that's how God is. That's how He is. That's why everyone of us is near and dear to God. Do not think you are an outcast. You are not. There is only one love, and that's God's Love. How else could it be, but unconditional? Because He naturally has our own interest at heart, He wants to draw all things back unto Himself.

That's the law He has made: the Law of Creation sends His great force out to create all things, but the law of His Love pulls all things back to Him. And so that pull which you feel at different times, sometimes more than others, is none other than God's great pull to draw you back—to draw each one of us back—without restriction, without condition, back home to Him. And so true friendship is based on the presence of God in a dynamic way, in a knowable way. That's the way back home to God. That's the spiritual law, and that's why you feel friendship for one another according to the presence of God felt in the friend, whether it is unconditional, or nearly so, or of another nature where there is possession, limitation, and restriction.

God's Love is Unconditional

With God, there are no restrictions, no matter what we do, no matter how evil we are, if you can call it that, or how much steeped in sin, which we are not. We are just steeped in a little delusion. We feel separated from God. That's all. The minute you remove that separation, there is no sin. God realizes that. He realizes that we are under His delusion—His creative delusory force of Satan—none other than duality, multiplicity, relativity.

In your meditations, when you go a little deep, where is delusion? It does not exist. In place of that we find the one love of the Infinite Father, without any ripples. You know that statement of Master's, when you are in the ripples of the mind, sometimes ordinary family love and personal love is like the ocean. One day everything is fine, the next day everything is not fine, like the boat rocking up and down on the sea.

You are a human being, but you stand on the shore. And you are a god because you feel God's unconditional Love, because there is no restlessness there. Unconditional Love—whether it is between friends, man and wife, or just acquaintances—it can develop into that friendship: unconditional love of God. So that's the key, that's the point we should remember in this subject, "Divine Love" or "The True Love:" that there is one God, and He has split Himself up into many, and He is seated in the hearts of each one of us. He wants to go back home, but He has given us free will to go back home or to stay out in this delusion.

As gods, we elect to go back home to Him. As human beings, we will stay awhile in this delusion, until we have had enough of it, and then we return home to God. True friendship, with its Divine Love, supersedes family love, and such limited forms of love, because these loves, as I have said, are conditioned—conditioned by selfishness, possession, and other outward conditions. True friendship is unconditioned.

Recalling the Master's Letter

I remember a letter Master once wrote me a long time ago from Portland, Oregon. This was when he first left Boston and came across the country; he went up to Alaska and then came down and started what we have now. I think the relationship with the guru is the greatest expression of true friendship, and I will point out to you, as I read the letter, just what we must avoid and what we must foster, if we are to enjoy true friendship with one another and, of course, with God.

In his letter written in 1925, he said, "I have found the law of love and reciprocal goodness are the strongest ties, the greatest impelling forces that make us responsible to one another."* Not what you can give the other one, not what you can get out of another person, but as he says, "the greatest impelling forces"—the law of love and reciprocal goodness. Why? Because God is seated in the hearts of each friend. "That's why," the Master goes on, "material binding is futile and meaningless—especially where there is a spiritual tie." The material binding between you and your friend will pass away. It's got to, but that spiritual bond of Divine love is eternal, because that's God himself.

So in your friendship, be sure, if you want it to last, that it has those qualifications. I think that is one of the

---
*See page 83 in this volume.

greatest letters I have received from the Master, because it lays it plainly before you. True friendship is on the spiritual plane. There can be great friendship on the material plane, but if it is backed up by the Divine consciousness by realizing that God is seated in the heart of each friend, then it is really true friendship, because it is eternal. The guru-disciple relationship is the greatest, because it is built wholly on the mutual desire to help one another and, by that union, to create a great flame of spirit flowing from that friendship, which others can follow back home to our one abode of light.

Going on a little bit, it is not necessary or possible to love all personally. That is one mistake I think we all make when we consider the Divine love of God unconditioned. Well, it's impossible to love all personally, but it doesn't mean that you realize this, when you feel the presence of God in all, that God is seated in the hearts of all, and as such, you are always ready to help them, when they need your help. When they need to be cheered up, when things are going wrong, they need a little solace. And sometimes when they are going wrongly on the material plane and they need material aid, it should be given according to your ability. That's what it means. It does not mean that you will be personally associated with everyone, because you would do nothing else. But you can always feel God in whomever you meet. It makes no difference when it is, you can feel Him, and you can lend that solace that you feel, the presence of God within. That will help that other friend or acquaintance whom you meet, until he, too, will gradually feel the presence of God through your goodness and through the fact that you have allowed God's love to flow through you.

We do nothing about it. God is the Doer. When He gets a channel, He uses it. That's spiritual law. That's the law we have to realize. So feel God in the hearts of all. How can you do it? Through Yoga. Lots of people say it's hard to do—every other person is their enemy. That's the way it is. I wouldn't want it that way, but that's what's going on all around. It's hard to say, "Just see God in the hearts of all, and you'll be all right." It's impossible to do that just from the words, but if you really practice Self-Realization Fellowship Yoga, which means Union, and attain the presence of God, then His love flows through you. Then you can feel God in the hearts of all. Feeling that, then you can know God is in all.

We must all feel and know that one eternal presence which we feel in all things, for that's Divine Love. Divine Love is what? Divine Love is the burning power of the consciousness of God's Presence, His Omniscience, His All-prevading Consciousness. Can you separate the burning power from the fire? Of course not. So Divine Love is the burning power, the fire of God's Consciousness. There is only one consciousness, and that's God Himself. So realize the burning power of God's Consciousness within yourself, then you can give it to others and be a friend to all. Do not feel you must take on all individuals in a definite way. This way you do a better job. You stimulate within others—because God is flowing through you—the ability to help them to feel the presence of God within.

Family Love Becomes Transmuted into Divine Love

I have a reference here from some of Master's works. Someone was complaining, "Why does the Lord give us families, if he doesn't want us to love them more than we love other people?" Now that's a good question. The family tie is very strong, but if you feel the love of God in your family, then you will be able to love them better, and there will be no restrictions. The love will be greater, and it will develop and change into Divine Love. You are not going to lose anything. You're not going to lose that daughter or son whom you love so much, or that husband or wife. You will not lose them. You will gain them more, because you will feel God in them.

So Master goes on to say, "By placing us in families, God affords us an opportunity to overcome selfishness and to find it easy to think of others." It is very difficult to think of others when you have a son or daughter you are attached to. It is very difficult. Break the attachment, and you will think more of your son or daughter. So Master goes on, "In friendship, He offers us a way to broaden further our sympathies. Even that is not the end. And the end is God Alone." God Alone. We must love God for Himself alone, not for what He can give us. Although we do utilize that aspect of love, we must love God alone for Himself alone. So we should continue to expand our love, until it becomes Divine, encompassing everyone everywhere.

Otherwise, how can we achieve oneness with God, the Father of all? "Thou shalt have no other Gods besides me." You might say, "Thou shalt have no other friends but me, because I am in all friends." These are the lessons we must learn from this lesson this morning.

Master's Rules for Friendship

Now a few rules. These rules were given by the Master. They are simple, but you will find if you obey them, your relationships with friends will be much better. The first and general rule is this: When friendship is not based on Divine Love, then it is blind and leads to conditions and restrictions. And even when that friendship is thwarted, it may lead to blind hate. I have seen it many times, because it was not based on unconditional, Divine Love. That's the first and greatest rule. If friendship is not based on that rule, then you will run into trouble; and it may go as far as to turn into blind hate. It is so without question of a doubt.

The other rules Master gives are these: Do not be sarcastic to a friend. Familiarity breeds contempt. And sometimes, when the friend is quite close to you, you might be sarcastic. But if you feel God in that friend, you will not be. Do not be sarcastic to friends. Do not flatter them, unless it is to encourage them. Do not placate them, unless it is to encourage them.

The next rule: Do not agree when they are wrong. That's a hard one. Say, "No sir, that is not right. I tell you because I love you so much." Do not flatter them. Do not agree when they are wrong. If I'm not sure who is wrong, I know I want to preserve that relationship in God with each one who comes to me—because that is of God—then I'm not going to blindly dive into that situation. But when I'm sure, then it's different, because it is difficult to discipline others we know. We all need it ourselves, and under certain conditions, we can do it. Fools argue, friends discuss. Sometimes I hear it going on in good shape. It's not discussion, it's arguing! So these are the rules that Master gives us. Now true friendship consists in being mutually useful. That's an important point.

The Guru-Disciple Relationship

Now we come to the guru-disciple friendship. This is the greatest thing, because this is the direct route to God through Divine Love, through God's unconditional love. It is a spiritual law, and I know a great many of you here have that relationship. You have that relationship because you want that unconditional love. And with that love you give Divine Love. You stir up a great flame of spirit because of the love which you have within yourself and with your guru.

And by that love, by the guru-disciple relationship, you help others, you set the example for others to follow back home to God. Master told me, "Let your life be an example for others to follow, where all will meet who live and do right." Who set the example? He set the example which I have tried to follow. That's the greatest friendship, because that's the spiritual law. And see what happens? Both go to God. Let that be the bond in your spiritual friendship.

The greatest is the guru-disciple relationship. Because what is the spiritual law of the guru-disciple relationship? The guru introduces his friend to God. He introduces his friend to the friend of all friends, that one eternal Father. That's the greatest relationship. That's the most wonderful thing.

In the *Autobiography,* I read a little bit about such a friendship which I should like to give you at this time. The friendship between the guru and the disciple—between Sri Yukteswar and his disciple, our Master, Paramahansa Yogananda. You remember when the Master first met Sri Yukteswar, Sri Yukteswar told him, "I give you my unconditional love. Will you give me the same unconditional love?" Master said, "I will love you eternally, Gurudeva." "Ordinary love is selfish, darkly rooted in desires and satisfactions. Divine Love is without condition, without change. The flux of the human heart is gone forever."

That's the restlessness of ordinary life at the transfixing touch of pure love. He added humbly—and this is the greatness of Sri Yukteswarji speaking to his disciple (Why could he speak to him that way? Because through his disciple, Paramahansa Yogananda, he saw God.), for this is what he said: "If ever you find me falling from the state of God Realization, please promise to put my head on your lap and help to bring me back to the Cosmic Beloved we both worship." That is Divine Love, unconditioned. I used to go to the Master with my head hanging down, ashamed of the many things I did. He would make no show of anything; "Come on in," he would say. That's Divine, unconditional love.

That's what you must have for your friend. You must feel within your friend the presence of God and never betray a friend, for that is the greatest sin. Worse than murder is the betrayal of a friend. The guru-disciple relationship is the greatest relationship to demonstrate the one true love, Divine Love.

And so, my true friend was our Master. These things are difficult to speak about, and it is unnecessary to speak about them. He knows whom He lets know. He knows whom God lets know. You will know when God lets you know. In true friendship like the guru-disciple relationship, each knows. Just like when you feel the presence of God, you know, and no one can take it away from you, because there is Divine Love in it. I will read to you (to express that) from one of Master's letters to me, to show you, and perhaps point out to you, just that true friendship in Divine Love.

He wrote this from Phoenix in 1930:

> God I care not for riches
> Nor for fame or pomp;
> But give me true friends!
> Even just one, if it be he
> Through whom I may behold Thee
> And whom I may trust and enjoy without,
>   As Thine image,
> E'er reflected in the mirror of my love.
> Ah wavelets of true friendship, heaven-born,
> Merge in Thy one ocean of vast Love!
> In the sea of friendship
> The meandering lost and prodigal souls
> Come back to their own one home.

Can there be a greater friend than that? That's an example of Divine friendship.

Chapter 5

Intellect versus Intuition

> *"To know the truth only intellectually is truly not to know it at all, because truth comes through intuition."* — Doctor Lewis, San Diego Temple, March 30, 1958.

When Jesus went into Jerusalem, palms were laid down in his honor, but it wasn't long before they crucified him. And so you see the lesson is that outward praise is not the goal; but what Jesus had was the kingdom of God, the kingdom of heaven within. That was his real power and his real treasure, so do not expect it in this worldly existence, as is clearly pointed out by Jesus' life. Having people proclaiming you is not the end; the end is oneness with God, and that has a great bearing on our subject this morning, "Intellect versus Intuition."

Intellect gives you knowledge by way of the senses and mind. But that is not always accurate; it is not always dependable; we all know that, and so we must realize that any premise established through the senses, mind and intellect, if it is wrong, it makes your whole reasoning—your whole deductive reasoning—wrong, does it not? So understand that. Do not depend upon the testimony of the senses, mind, and intellect. It is not dependable. You see illustrations of this all the time.

One special instance of this I can tell you. As we were coming in from Twenty-Nine Palms one day with the Master, quite some time ago now, in the distance we saw a great cloud of smoke. As we rode along we began to wonder and to suggest what it would be up in Banning. We rode along watching it; and before we got any where near the town, we realized it was not smoke, but it was a cloud of dust which had swirled up from the desert.

So you see, the testimony of the senses is not accurate, and the premise which we had established proved entirely wrong. Understand that. Be careful of the premises which you establish through the testimony of the senses, mind, and intellect. To know the truth only intellectually is truly not to know it at all, because truth comes through intuition. If our intuition had been established there, we would have known that the cloud of smoke was dust, no matter what the senses led us to believe. This is true. Understand that truth is perceived and known only through the intuition. It comes of itself; it does not depend upon sensation or any outward form of testimony or reason. When you know through intuition, you know; and no one can change that. That's the difference between intellect and intuition.

In the *Autobiography of a Yogi,* there is a story about a celebrated pundit who came to Swami Sri Yukteswarji. This pundit knew all about the Mahabharata, the Gita, the Commentaries of Lord Shankara, the Upanishads, the Vedas and so on. As he was talking away extolling things, suddenly Master's Master began to laugh; and he asked the pundit, "Have you applied any of these teachings in your life? Have you any realization?" The man said, "No, I haven't." So you see, there's the difference between theoretical knowledge and realization.

This man was very learned, but he knew nothing through intuition about the presence within himself of God, truth, and reality. So we must understand not to be hoodwinked, so to speak, by the testimony of the senses, mind, and intellect. We have to utilize them in this life naturally, but this life is not reality. It passes away. Anything that is born must pass away; but within us is a consciousness and a presence of God which does not pass away. Having that you have all things. Understand that. That's why meditation is so important.

Meditation is for the purpose of consciously contacting the presence of God as you understand it within. That's why intuition is so important, because intuition does not come through outward testimony, but through the conscious contact of God within. God knows all things through intuition; we know things through sensation, mind and intellect plus intuition. He knows immediately without the agency of any outward testimony of senses, mind, or intellect or anything else. Intuition is the all-knowing power of the soul. It knows completely, immediately. It does not depend upon anything else. How do you realize that you exist? Do you think about it? "How do I exist?" Or look around? You know you exist through the intuition of the soul within.

So much for intellect. Now about intuition. As I have said, intuition is related to the Sanskrit word *agama:* "that which comes" of itself, that which does not depend upon any outside agency, and so intuition is the power of God within you—the power of your own soul, which knows without the agency of sight, hearing, taste, smell, touch, intellect, deductive reasoning or inference. It knows completely by itself.

From *The Autobiography Of a Yogi,* we read that almost everyone has had "hunches." Didn't those hunches come true? You couldn't shake them. Why? Because they came through the intuition of the soul. Not all of them are intuitional experiences: some are simply machinations of the mind, so to speak. But once in a while you will have something that will stick; and it comes true, because it comes from intuition.

Stilling the Mind

Now we have a testimony about intuition in the *Autobiography of a Yogi,* where we read, "Intuition is soul guidance, appearing naturally in man during those instances when his mind is calm." Don't you think meditation is necessary? With the mind running this way, hither and yon, how can intuition get in? How can it operate? It cannot. So realize, intuition comes when the mind is still. There will be flashes of it when there are no thoughts. "When the thoughts have gone to rest," as the Master used to say, "That's the time I see God best." So that's when intuition comes.

Intuition is soul guidance appearing naturally in man, but we don't give it a chance. We are so taken up with this restless mind, and the doings of this worldly existence, and a million other things, poor intuition can not operate. But it will operate, if you still the waves of the mind. And so that is what we read, going on a little further, "The human mind, freed from the disturbances or 'static' of restlessness ..."—realize this; these are the Master's own words—"is empowered to perform [through its antenna of intuition] all functions of complicated radio mechanisms—sending as well as receiving thoughts and tuning out undesirable ones."*

We have within us a radio receiving broadcasting station which is exact, which operates without fault, if we tune out thoughts and those things which disturb us. Because we are a ray of the Infinite Omniscience of God who knows all things, His great power—His all seeing universal power of sight, the universal power of healing—is in us. It is through that force that God's radio operates and knows all things. We have that, but we clutter it up with worldly thoughts and consciousness.

Let us understand this. These are the Master's words,

---

*Doctor Lewis refers to a discussion on intuition which takes place in the chapter entitled "The Cauliflower Robbery" in the *Autobiography of a Yogi.*

"As the power of a radio-broadcasting station is regulated by the amount of ... current [through which it operates] ..."—that's the power of the radio station, and so we read in the *Autobiography* here—"As the power of a radio-broadcasting station is regulated by the amount of electrical current it can utilize, so the effectiveness of a human radio depends on ... ," yes, power, but what kind of power? Will power. And so when you still the waves of your mind, and in that silence within, if you use the power of your will, then you can operate the radio station which God has given to you. And so just to finish, "As the power of the radio broadcasting station is regulated by the amount of electrical current it can utilize, so the effectiveness of the human radio depends on the degree of will power possessed by each individual."*

The will power is the thing. How do you think God created this universe, just by sitting down and thinking about it? No, He put His will into it. And so, if you want to change through meditation, put your will power into it. Sit there. Make your mind as calm as you can; but sit there and use your will, in the best way you can, to reach the goal. You will have conscious communion with God, and you will know He is guiding you in every action. That's what we can do, but we can do it, not through intellect, not through sensation nor mind, but through the power of intuition within us, the power of God within us, the soul's power.

Now, let me give an illustration about intellectual knowledge versus intuitional knowledge or realization. In everyday activity, for instance, you can know about a theoretical aspect of something. Let's say you want to make a cake. You read all about how to do this, but when you make the

---

*This passage illustrates how Doctor would treat his Guru's words: he would repeat a portion of it, expand on that, repeat another portion, expand further, and so on, each time deeping the listener's understanding and appreciation.

cake, don't you find it different from reading about making that cake?

In every walk of life, get away from depending on this outward agency of mind, senses and intellect. Turn toward the intuitional power of God within you, because intuition is different, realization is different, than theory. You can know all about a thing; you can read all about it; you can understand all about it, but it will be different when you taste that thing, when you feel that thing through intuition.

That brings me to this one rule, which I would like to read to you: "No matter how much a thing is intensely described or how many comparisons given, you cannot realize it until you become one with that thing or situation." In studying all about my profession, I studied really hard and received good marks, but when I came to practice it and to become one with the situation, it was entirely different. That's the difference between theory and realization, the difference between intellect and intuition.

Comparing the Two Approaches

Now let us go on just a little further and compare conceptions of God. That's what we are really interested in. We are here for one purpose. And that's to know about God, because that's the thing that is going to save us. So let us consider a conception of God, first intellectually and then intuitionally.

We can all say after reading the Bible, in Saint John, "In the beginning was the Word, the Word was with God, the Word was God." We can all say that. Light, Sound, and Feeling: remembering those three things, we can say "God is Light," which is an aspect of the Word. Yes, science has shown all things come from Light. Everything can be reduced to Light. God is Light. That's knowing that intellectually.

We can also say, "God is sound." God is the great Holy Vibration, the sound of His Cosmos running. And in the

Bible, we read many places about that sound: the trumpet sound, the sound of many waters, the voice of God. And our so conception can be an intellectual one.

We can read about it, we can understand it intellectually, and then take the feeling aspect. We read Jesus' words, "The peace that passeth all understanding." We know those things, and we also perhaps realize Jesus has said, "Eye hath not seen nor ear heard the things which God has prepared for those who feel for Him who love Him." We can know that theoretically.

Swami Ram said, "Peace like a river flows through me. Peace like a river flows through me." Lord Shankara said, "I am He. I am He. Blessed Spirit, I am He." So we know our conception of God can be intellectual, but that's quite different from an intuitional conception of God, where we know it though feeling and tasting the Presence of God.

And so when we say, "God, thou art the Creator of all things; Thou hast made all things," we will not only know that theoretically, we will feel our consciousness expanded from this limited body through the great ocean of God's Presence throughout all creation not in imagination, but in reality. That's our conception of God as the Creator intuitionally.

And then we can take the Word with its Light, its great Sound and the great Touch of God's Presence. And when we see the Light, we say, "God is Light." We look within in the spiritual eye, and we see the spiritual eye as reality here, not just theoretically. We see perhaps an expanded state of our consciousness, wherein the great spiritual light is spread all over. That's realization.

That's an intuitional conception of God; that's knowing God really. Or we can hear the Cosmic Sound, not knowing it theoretically, we can hear it. We can not only hear it; we can feel it vibrating through us. That's touching God. That's our conception of God as the Holy Vibration. Intuitionally, in reality, we have tasted God. And the greatest of all of these is the feeling aspect of God, which we know through our intuition, when we feel as Jesus said, "Peace that passeth all understanding," or as Swami Ram [Tirtha] said, "Peace like a river flows through me." Lord Shankara said, "I am He. I am He."

Then you not only talk about it, you not only theorize about it, but you feel one with that. Now that's the conception of God—no, not in theory, not in imagination, but in reality. And those who meditate and make that conscious contact with God and feel Him will have that conception of God in reality. They will taste God. As Master used to say, "You can talk all about sugar; you can describe its crystalized form, but until you taste it, you do not know sugar, do you?" Realize that.

Until you taste God through the intuition of the soul, through the power of God within you, you do not really know Him. When you taste Him, you know Him in reality. Now that will give you a comparison of the intellectual conception of God and the intuitional conception of tasting God which is so real.

Developing Intuition

And finally, let us talk about how to develop this wonderful thing called intuition. How do you develop intuition? Practice yoga. Yoga means union. Don't think the thoughts will cease by your saying, "Cease now." They won't; they are too deeply instilled within us.

We have to practice yoga scientifically; then, when the thoughts have ceased, what happens? Then comes, in the silence within, the intuition of the soul. As Master has said, "Not in books, not in theoretical knowledge, is the Kingdom of God's consciousness known, but in the Silence within." When the thoughts have gone to rest, the intellect has stopped, so to speak, and then in that Silence is the Infinite awareness of God.

And what is that Infinite awareness of God? That's the intuition by which God knows all things. In that Infinite awareness within you and within me, when the thoughts have gone to rest, you will find two things which constitute the Omniscience of God within and which is in all things. First is the Universal Power of Sight to see above, beneath, in front, behind, all around. That's the power of intuition, the *Kutastha,* as it is called in Hindu philosophy or in the Vedas. We also will have the Universal Power of Feeling, the Consciousness to feel above, beneath, in front, behind instantly. That is known as *Bishnu,* the Universal Power of Feeling.

Those two things constitute God's great Consciousness, His power that we will find through the practice of yoga in the inner awareness within. You cannot exhaust it. Realize that. The Kingdom of God is within; it is knowable in the silence within. It is knowable, not through mind, or intellect, but through intuition. And so our Master has said, and the Bible says, "Be explorers in the Kingdom of God, be explorers in the Kingdom of Consciousness." Know God in reality.

I have another reference from the *Autobiography of a Yogi*. It is this: "The goal of yoga science is to calm the mind." That's right; if we could calm the mind, then the intuition of God within us would flow naturally. But what a job to calm the mind! We have to do it, but yoga helps you very much. Yoga is scientific. The goal of yoga science is to calm the mind, that without distortion it may hear the infallible council of the inner voice.

So do not be satisfied to be a theoretical devotee of God. You don't have to be. Don't be satisfied with that, but be a realized devotee, wherein you feel His power within you, wherein you are not satisfied to talk about God or read about God—you are not going to give up until you feel His Presence, which you can, through right meditation and devotion to God. God must answer, because He is us; He's within us, our own thoughts and consciousness are God, our own consciousness is His Consciousness. Our own breath, He has given us. So let us realize. Let us not be satisfied just to be theoretical followers of God, but to be realized followers, realized devotees, who are not satisfied until God comes to us.

Who wants to talk about God? We don't want that, that's not enough. We are in trouble. We have problems: all of us have problems, and we are not going to be satisfied unless God comes to us, unless we know Him, not theoretically, but intuitionally. When He comes into us, then, if by chance, His Grace falls upon us and we receive the vision of His face, then we have all things. And that vision does not come through all the learning of all the books in the world. It comes when the heart is pure gold. It comes to the pure in heart, to the simple, but [only] to those who love God. When that comes, then we will know God really. We will be one with Him.

I'll close with Lahiri Mahasaya's great words, for all those who really want God not intellectually, but intuitionally. He said, and this applies to everyone, don't think that some get off, and that others do not. Everybody has a hard job, but keep at it, whatever you do, in your meditations. If you feel, "I'm getting nowhere," if you keep on and practice, you will get somewhere.

I have proved it myself, otherwise I wouldn't tell you these things. Many in this room, as I talk to them, they have said the same thing. Even though we seem to be getting nowhere, we are progressing, because anything done to please God pays the greatest dividend. And so when you meditate, keep on, keep on, keep on; and then in Lahiri Mahasaya's great words, "One day;" and this is true, absolutely true. All I can tell you is my own experience. All you can tell me is your experience. That's all you can attest to. But I say, Lahiri Mahasaya's words, "Striving, striving, striving, one day the Divine goal, the Vision of God."

Chapter 6
The Cosmic Dream

Hollywood Temple
January 3rd, 1960

The subject this morning, "The Cosmic Dream," is in a sense a very difficult one, because if you try to discuss your own dream with someone, you will not get very far. When you wake up, the dream passes away, and you return into outward consciousness. This shows that the dream has no real existence.

When you wake up, so to speak, into this waking consciousness in which you are operating now, where is the dream? But when you were in the dream, it was pretty real, was it not? You tasted, and you smelt, and you got chased, or you chased someone else. There is no end to what can happen in your dream, but the thing to remember is this: when you wake up, when you come into waking consciousness, the dream disappears. Then you know it was a product of your own waking consciousness. That's the important thing to remember in order to understand this subject, "The Cosmic Dream."

I remember the Master told me many times, "Always remember the illustration of the dream, and then you can more easily understand this Cosmic Dream." Now it is the same exactly, the only difference is that in this little dream, so to speak, your consciousness, separated from the universal consciousness, has produced the dream. In other words, your invisible thought becomes visible, so to speak, in your dream. And yet when you wake up and come back into this one waking consciousness, where is your dream?

Now that brings up a rule which you must never forget: to break a dream—whether it be your individual dream or the great universal dream of God—you must wake up into the original consciousness which has produced the dream. Therefore, in the same way as you break your own dream, when you wake up into ordinary waking consciousness, in order to break the cosmic dream, you must wake up into that consciousness which is producing it, Cosmic Consciousness, or God the Father.

Sooner or later, you will be awakened by Divine Mother into that Consciousness which has produced all this Creation. Realize that the rule is simple: you break whatever the dream is—individual or Cosmic—by waking up into that state of consciousness which has produced it; in one instance, your own individual waking consciousness; or in the other instance, the universal Presence of God as Cosmic Consciousness.

Waking up in that, you will see the dream pass away—just as your own dream passes away. You wake up. How real it was! Suddenly you wake up, and you see it—if you can hold it a little bit—sliding off. So, with this dream of the world, it is exactly the same. You'll understand it only if you wake up into that consciousness which is producing it: God's Cosmic Consciousness.

Now the saints and sages of India in ancient times have likened this universe to the materialized thought of God; that is, this universe is like the nature of a dream. And now I understand why the Master was so adamant in impressing me to remember my own dream state.

Because you will find, as you meditate more and become more and more divorced from this worldly consciousness, that you will wake up in the Presence of God. You will see and know this as a dream, more so than you know your own dream when you wake up in ordinary consciousness. That's why I am so happy. At least I listened; and secondly, I followed what he told me to do.

Breaking the Cosmic Dream

The breaking of the dream finally has to come through the Grace of God, but you have to prepare yourself so that you receive that Grace. You ask, "How?" By following yoga: Raja Yoga. It simply means the science of uniting your separated consciousness from God to its real home, or to Cosmic Consciousness. We are that, but we do not realize it, and so we seem apart; you're there and I'm here; the world is there and seems so real.

The sense of touch is the worst thing, because when you feel a thing, it's pretty hard to realize that it isn't as it is. But it's nothing but vibrating light atoms, and you feel it's so wonderful. Other things you can supersede easily, but the sense of touch is very difficult. The other thing to remember is that this body is not your dream; it's the dream of God.

And so psychologically you can break your own dream, and you can feel apart from this body. Nothing worries you a bit. Why? Because you have broken the psychological dream, but when you wake up and feel good, there's the body; there is everybody and all the trouble waiting for you. Why? It is a fact, because you haven't broken the Cosmic Dream, so then you get busy and try harder. One day, God says, "Come on, you've tried hard enough, you've had trouble enough." And your soul will say, "Amen." Then he breaks the Cosmic Dream, and you say, "My Lord, what have I been fiddling around with this ego consciousness for?"

It is the ego consciousness that causes all this to be so real. Do you understand that? It's the consciousness that you think you are the Doer of this thing, instead of realizing that God is the Doer. Sometimes you get into all sorts of messes, until you realize by these troubles that there is something wrong. Then, in your misery, you turn to the Lord and you say, "Get me out of this, break this dream. 'From This Dream Lord, Will you Wake Me?'" And He says, "All right, come on." Just like that. Just like you break your own dream, but you have to prepare yourself. You have to, by the practice of yoga, know the Presence of God, know His Reality as Peace and Bliss, and the undifferentiated Consciousness of Light. You have to know that. Then He can break the Dream, but not until then.

The Material Thought of God

And so this Cosmic Dream, remember, is like your own dream, only it is simply the materialized thought of God. Instead of your own thought projected from the subconscious mind, it is a projection of the thought of God. As it says in Genesis, "God created Heaven and Earth, and they were without form and void." Well, where were they? They were in His thought, that's all. And then when He created Light, he created electronic energy: vibration, the Great Cosmic Energy, the Om Sound, the Amen of our Bible, the Om of the Hindus, the Amin of the Mohammedans.

He created that vibration, that Light, and projected that Light energy as a motion picture which produced this thing which seems so real. It is not real. It is not as it seems. Now, we do that same thing in our little dream. We have all these thoughts stored up and added to every day and every minute in the subconsciousness. Then through the law of projection, duality, we pass that energy through the little films and project onto the screen of consciousness our dream. We do the same thing as God does, only He does it in a far greater measure.

The thing to remember in this Cosmic Dream is that it is the materialized thought of God. You have the Scriptures,

"God created Heaven and Earth, and they were without form and void." And then He created Light; then he energized, so to speak, these thoughts which he had—which took millions of years, according to our sense of time—to produce the different creations, the universes. And then he projected that light through these films of thought and has given us this universe, this creation. Now that's what the cosmic dream is; but it doesn't seem as simple as that, and it seems so real, because the ego is attached to it.

If we can get rid of the ego, throw it out, then we can feel that we are not the Doer, and we can understand much easier. But as long you think you are the Doer, you cannot do a thing. God is the One; He's the One, and that's the hardest thing to realize.

It is scientific. You do so much, and you get so much evolution.* You do so much more, you get that much more evolution. And when you do enough, the ego is eliminated. And then God has freedom to come into you and say, "Now you see I'm the sole Doer. Thou shalt have no other Gods before me." It's just what He means, but how difficult it is to say, "Lord, now you take care of things." Because in the next minute, there you are at it again. These are facts. You can get away from them. I have found it so; and if you are sincere and truthful, you will say, "That's right, Amen." And these things are facts.

Just a reference at this time from our Master's writings. He says things which take a long time to understand. (I'm all right, I haven't been drinking. Sometimes God is so wonderful, you just forget everything. Instead of standing straight, you are apt to fall over. Well, that's all right.†) Now let's go on with this reference: that there is one underlying noumenon, and that's God's Presence. The underlying noumenon is the greatest thing. If you can understand

---

*Doctor Lewis is referring to Kriya Yoga.

†In his high state of realization, sometimes Doctor would be overwhelmed with Divine Bliss causing him to sway at the pulpit.

that, and know that you are not this body, but vibrating Light of God. Science has shown these things; I'll come to it in just a moment.

"The whole universe is the materialized thought of the Creator. This heavy, earthly clod, floating in space, is a dream of God. He made all things out of His Consciousness, even as man in his dream consciousness reproduces and vivifies a creation with its creatures."* These are our Master's words, these are words of Truth.

God first created the earth as an idea. I spoke to you about Genesis; and then, He created this Holy Vibration to produce those things as solids, liquids, gases, etc. First, He produced the Atom, and then on that He built all things, until finally He has the Creation. He did that, how? By His Will; and so likewise do we, although we do not realize it, because our will is there, will hidden underneath in the subconsciousness. "When He withdraws His Will," the Master says, "the earth will disintegrate into energy. Energy will dissolve into consciousness, and the earth idea will disappear from objectivity."

Doesn't your dream do the same thing? So it will be, when you wake up in God. This dream, which seems so real, will disappear from objectivity, but only when you have become that consciousness which has produced the dream, Cosmic Consciousness. We are that, only we don't realize it.

And so from thought this whole material universe has come. As I have pointed out, by creative energy activating the thought producing the great cosmic sound of Om, or the Great Holy Vibration, the Spirit, the Comforter of which Jesus spoke, from that projecting the Light, this thing material universe has come. Science substantiates the dream nature of the universe.

This isn't just some idea; this has been shown and proven

---

*From the chapter, "Materializing a Palace in the Himalayas" in the *Autobiography of a Yogi*.

by science. Science has shown and is showing that matter is always changing and resolving first into electromagnetic force and finally into light. Think of it! Heavy metals that seem so heavy and solid are but light atoms vibrating at a certain rate of speed.

We have the testimony of Eddington.* Eddington says that matter is ever becoming energy, and energy resolves into light. However solid it may appear to us in this physical world, which operates under the principle of relativity and duality, it is not as real as it appears to be. We have become attached to it, because we do not see with the Cosmic Consciousness of God; otherwise, we wouldn't see this book as we can see it now, but we, through intuition, would see it as the vibrating light of God.

Meditation is the Key

Now don't think these things are far-fetched. Meditate; and you will be able to prove it. If you don't meditate, you will never know. You have to do your part. The Master used to say, "I can tell you what to do, but you have to do it." And so we must do those things. So science substantiates these things and, also, substantiates the motion picture aspect. Even heavy metals under the electron microscope are seen as, what? Vibrating points of light. Think of it, heavy metals! And the latest in 1960 is, or perhaps 1959, is that mind has been found to be very fast moving particles of light.

That's why if you can control your mind, you can travel any distance instantaneously. So things are not as they seem to be. These things have been shown scientifically, not just in imagination. Not long ago light has been taken, it has been synthesized into electromagnetic force and, finally, into matter. How can you doubt these things? It has been

---

*Stanley Arthur Eddington (1882–1944) was a well-known English astronomer and physicist.

shown done by Dr. Oldenberg of Harvard University. His subject was, "The Production of Particles from Radiation, Gamma Rays, and Positrons." So we are way behind the times fooling around with this outer consciousness. Let us meditate and know, know that this Cosmic Dream is the creation of the thought of God, and that even time and space have been shown to be unreal.

There is no time and space when you sit quiet in meditation; if you haven't meditated, try it. Time and space evaporate. Even Kant said that quite a few years ago: time and space do not exist except as attributes of the mind. Let us realize that we are not this body. We are the vibrating Light and Love and Energy of God which cannot be hurt, or be sick or sinful, is ever-existent, always was, and always will be; that's what we must know. And we can know it by proving that we can break this Cosmic Dream.

Now you can't dematerialize God's dream, but He can. Just as you dissolve your dream, so God can dissolve His other dream. And we have to let Him do it. That's the point. He follows a Divine pattern.

God would not send to us an agent as our Master unless it could be done by each one of us. In fact, that is why God sends the sages and the saints to show us it can be done. What do we do? Nothing, many of us. Why not follow them? It's not difficult; only we have to follow, that's all.

Attachment brings Sorrow

Now going on just a little bit about being attached to this Cosmic Dream. We are attached emotionally to this Cosmic Dream, and the result is sorrow, trouble. Master used to say this, "Change your attitude towards this Cosmic Dream." He used to say, "Don't take life too seriously." I was very serious-minded, and I didn't like that; he would say, "Don't pay too much attention to it." "We are here today and gone tomorrow."

Just before he passed away he said, "Remember when we first met, how wonderful it was, the love which we felt?

I said "Yes, Sir."

He said, "Life's a dream, isn't it?"

I said, "It sure is."

He said, "Where is your father? Where is my father? They're gone."

I said, "Yes, they are."

"But isn't that love the same?" he asked.

I said, "Yes, Sir."

He said, "As we started, let us finish."

It was he who gave me a taste of that Cosmic Consciousness of God's Love, and I never left it. By the Grace of God, somehow I hung on; and you all can do the same thing. "As we started, let us finish" in that One love of the Infinite which is none other than Cosmic Consciousness.

And so he also said this, he said, "Even though this life is a dream, even though we are here today and gone tomorrow," he said, "but the candles that you are lighting and burning in your Father's Home will light your path here and hereafter." Your Father's home is that home of Light and Energy of Cosmic Consciousness. You may not see that you are lighting them, but every time you meditate and feel the Presence of God, you are lighting a candle in that Infinite home of Light. That is one of the greatest things he has written to me.

Our Father's Home is the home of Light and energy beyond time and space, in which there is no trouble, no conflict, no sorrow, only God Alone, Infinite, unending. You cannot drain the great ocean of Bliss, so to speak, for it is perfect peace and joy. That's where we belong, even while in this existence here. If we can not prove this while living here, what's the good of it? What good is yoga, unless by yoga we can prove our immortality? We can do that, and we will do that, because sometime God is going to do it for us, but let's help Him out a little bit and do our part.

In this Cosmic Dream, our attitude should be that God is the Doer. If we could just somehow realize that and know that One Consciousness, we would have no more difficulty. We try to do it ourselves. Let us throw the Ego out, and we can, because God will never forsake us, if we will just do our part and try. Difficulties come, because we do not understand that we are in this Cosmic Dream of God, and we do not understand how to break it. But Master came to give us the ways and the means to know that One Consciousness from which this Cosmic Dream has come, knowing it just as your own dream breaks when you wake up, so this Cosmic Dream will pass away.

There will be no more sorrow. Jesus says that: "My Kingdom is not of this world." It is of the Light and Love of God. We must get into that Kingdom somehow, we must somehow break this Cosmic Dream. Remember once more the unequivocal law that you can break any dream, if you can understand and merge in the consciousness which has produced it. Merge in God's Consciousness. It's waiting for you; it's there, if we will but try just a little more. Keep on trying. From our Master's book, *The Master Said*,* a reference at this time to substantiate these things of which I have been speaking. "Life is a great dream of God. One of them [the students] inquired, 'If it is only a dream, then why is pain so real?'" This is what the Master said, "A dream head struck against a dream wall causes dream pain. A dreamer does not realize the falseness of a dream until he awakens. So the dualities of the Cosmic Dream cannot be known until a man wakes up in God and ceases to dream delusion."

How soon the ordinary dream passes away when you awaken in the morning! Just once taste the Consciousness of God, the Cosmic Consciousness, and this dream will be just the same. Such is God's Love for His Children. Let us

---

*First Edition, 1952; Reissued by Self-Realization Fellowship as *Sayings of Yogananda*.

realize our Master's Words. Meditation is the way, through Raja Yoga, to first attain the Presence of God, and then by full surrender.

That's the point which is so hard, because we think we are the Doer. We have to break that Ego Consciousness. First, attain the Presence of God; and then by full surrender, when there is no other consciousness in you, no other vibration of any consciousness except what you truly are, then you naturally merge through the Grace of God and become one with Him as Cosmic Consciousness of God. These are eternal truths. All the scriptures attest to them. Let us understand them.

Remember, the cause of sorrow is Ego Consciousness, the duality of Ego Consciousness with its blinding and binding power. How binding, and how much it blinds us! That's the trouble, but we can break it. Breaking that, we will understand reality of the One Cosmic Consciousness of which we are a part. We will understand God as the sole Doer.

Understanding that, how can the ego exist? It cannot exist. It has no place to go, if we realize and understand the One Father. Master said this wonderful thing, which I found in one of his older lectures. He says, "It is our own sense of our own importance which makes this world seem so real." Think of it. If you didn't realize, or think you realize, how big and important you are, you wouldn't be half so hurt. But if you can think that it is God who is the Doer, then you realize that you have no importance at all except as His Consciousness. These are immortal truths which the Master has given us.

Remember, the Cosmos is a varied expression of the One Power: Light, light vibrating at different rates of vibration, but guided by Divine Intelligence. Ordinary light is nothing we want, but God's Intelligence is perceived in the action of the Light, producing the light and shadows of this Cosmic Dream. This is what we want to know. Meditation is the way to understand these things, because by meditation, we supersede the ordinary faculties and powers of ego consciousness. We replace those by the unending, immortal power of the soul which comes through intuition.

The Role of Intuition

It is through intuition that we can break the Cosmic Dream, not by reason, not by mind, not by intellect. No matter how great it seems, you cannot understand the cosmic dream, but intuition can. The pure in heart, the humble, the simple, shall know God. Why? Because their intuition is developed. The capacity to break the cosmic dream through intuition is not interfered with by things of Spirit, but by ego consciousness. That is what we must understand.

We must through intuition know the one eternal substance from which all things come. It cannot be known by reason or intellect. It can easily be known by affection and love as the intuition of the soul. There is one supreme substance. Master has said, "Without question of a doubt, there is no difference whatsoever between Bliss Consciousness and God Consciousness." That does not mean just a little happiness. That means the Bliss of God's Presence, His Love. There is no difference.

The moment that you feel that in your heart welling up, hold on to it. That's the Presence of God. And little by little, adding a little bit to it, soon it will be all things. Master's words are most wonderful. He also said in his *Autobiography Of A Yogi,* the following: "Long continued concentration on the liberating spiritual eye has enabled the yogi to destroy all delusions concerning matter and its gravitation weight."* Because this is the seat of spiritual perception, the seat of Intuition, not the tip of the nose.

Jesus said, "If thine eye be single, thy whole body shall

---

*From the chapter "On the Law of Miracles" in the *Autobiography of the Yogi.*

be full of light."* He didn't mean the tip of the nose; he meant this eye here. [Doctor points to the Spiritual Eye.] Realize these things. Follow your yoga. Follow it intelligently. Therefore, he sees the universe, the yogi who penetrates the spiritual eye here. He sees the universe as an essentially undifferentiated mass of Light, but in that Light, what you feel in that Light is indescribable!

Jesus said, "The eye hath not seen, nor ear heard the things, which the Lord has prepared for those who love Him." Who want Him, that's all. Those who want Him that much, who never give up, will know and break the Cosmic Dream; breaking that, you will realize you always were, always will be, there is no separation between you, you are a part of Cosmic Consciousness.

And I'll close by just a word from one of Master's books, which is most wonderful, and I hope that you will always remember this last passage, in which he says, speaking of how quickly we may be released by God's Grace from the delusions of Maya, "At times it seems we will never get out of it." That is not true, for he goes on, "In this world we seem to be immersed in a sea of troubles. Then the Divine Mother comes and shakes us, awakening us from this terrible dream, that every man sooner or later will have that liberating experience. You see a child in bed, moving about, dreaming, what do you do? You shake him, wake him up into this waking consciousness. And so God will come, when we really want Him enough. He will shake us just that way. We will say, 'I was dreaming; I didn't realize what I was.'"

---

*Matthew 6:22.

Photographs from the
Family Album

Mildred Margaret Wentworth in 1915

Minott White Lewis about 1915

Wentworth residence, Samoset Road, S. Duxbury, Mass

Lewis residence, Elder Brewster Road, S. Duxbury, Mass

Dr. and Mrs. Minott Lewis, September 2, 1916. Wedding Day at Wentworth residence.

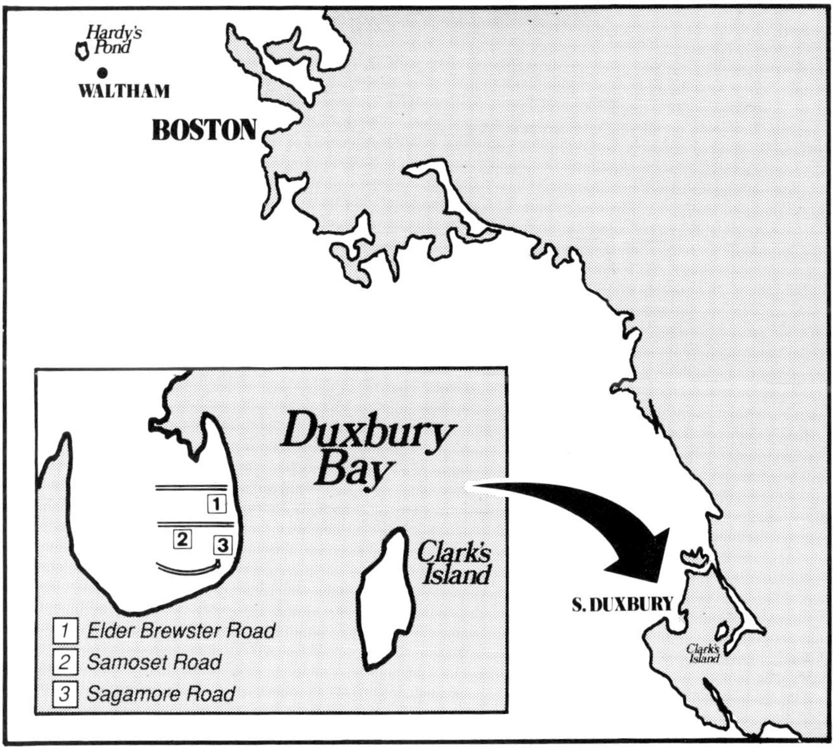

Home of Doctor and Mrs. Lewis (Sagamore Road) where Yogananda visited in the stories "The Master Rescues Doctor's Health" and "Enveloped in a Blue Light".

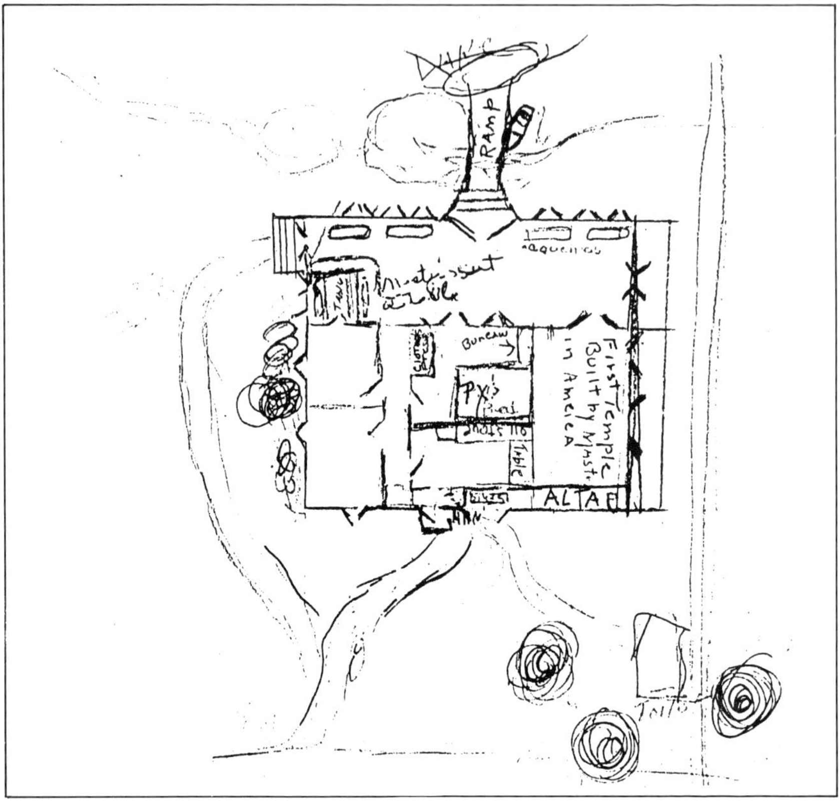

Sketch of Waltham Hermitage, 1922

Swami Yogananda atop Waltham Hermitage

Swami Yogananda and Mrs. Lewis early 1920's

Paramahansa Yogananda with Doctor and Mrs. Lewis in the 1940's

Doctor and Mildred Lewis, Encinitas, California, 1948

Paramahansa Yogananda with Doctor and Mrs. Lewis visiting the Redwoods in Northern California

Boat Ride: Paramahansa Yogananda with Mrs. Lewis and other disciples, Southern California

Paramahansa Yogananda and Dr. Lewis on the boat outing

Mildred Lewis, Borrego, 1960's

Dr. Lewis in front of the Hollywood Temple, late 1940's

Dr. Lewis playing the organ at the San Diego Temple

Mrs. Lewis in Hawaii 1978

Top Right:
Mildred Lewis at San Diego
Temple India Night, 1984

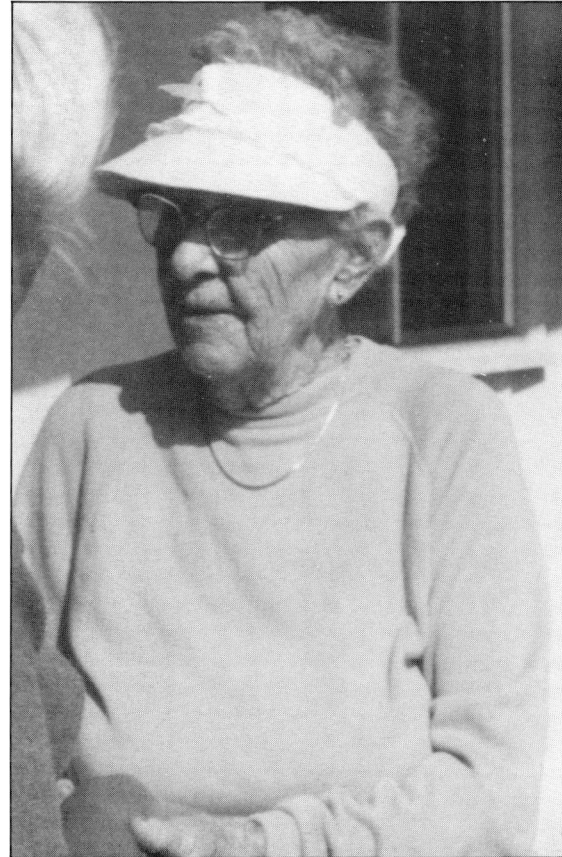

Mildred Lewis,
Borrego, 1981

Borrego Retreat, Borrego Springs, California

One of Mama Lewis' favorite pictures of Doctor, near Borrego

Memorial Plaque Commemorating the Lewis Chapel, Borrego, November 1, 1969

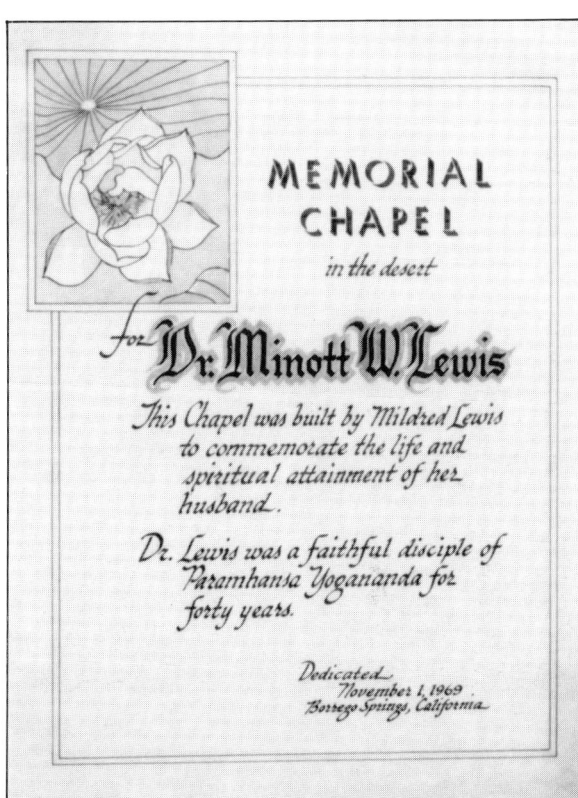

Dedication Day, Borrego

Entrance to Lewis Chapel, Borrego Springs, California

Inside view of Chapel altar showing meditation bench used by Doctor from 1920

Mrs. Lewis at her residence, San Diego Temple Grounds

Mildred Lewis, last picture, San Diego, 1988

Mama at the Harmonium

Doctor at the Hollywood Temple

The Master with Doctor and Mrs. Lewis

Dr. Lewis after Sunday Lecture San Diego Temple, 1960

Dr. and Mrs. Lewis at their S. Duxbury residence, 1943

Serampore
Dpr. 223, Ashar 7
Cor 21st June 1922

From Swami Srijukteshwar Giriji Maharaj,
President Sadhu sabha.
To Dr. M. W. Lewis D. M. D.
253 Elm Street, Lewis building Davis Sqr
West Somerville (mass) U.S.America.

SADHU SABHA
THE Executive Committee OF
SADHUMANDAL
(The Association of Sages.)

President—Srimat Swami Srivukteshwar Giri Jiu Maharaj.

Vice-Presidents—Swami Yogananda Giri Jiu, B.A., Roy Radha Charan Pal Bahadur.

Secretaries—Roy Atul Chandra Chowdhary, Sj. Ananda Mohan Lahiri M.A.

Editors—Swami Dhirananda Giri, M A., Sj. Nilananda Chatterji, M.A.

Upadeshakas—Swami Satyanand Giri. B.A., Sj. Upendra Mohan Chowdhury Kabibhushan.

Managers—Sj. Manamatha Nath Karar, Sj. Fatakrishna Ghosh.

Trustees—The Honorable Maharaja Sir Manindra Chandra Nandy, K.C.I.E. of Kashimbazar, and the selected office-bearers.

My Dear Doctor,

Yours of the 9th May is to hand. I heartily congratulate that you have advanced so much in spiritual consciousness and appriciated the real truth of the religion. Innumerable thanks to our Almighty Father through whose blessings my disciple Swami Yogananda has become a help to you. If our Sadhu Sabha gets a Home for Satsanga at your place, I shall be extremely glad to be with you there, and enjoy a pleasant trip with your company round the world. With my whole heart's love—

I remain,
Very sincerely Yours,

Letter from Swami Sri Yukteswar, 1922

Chapter 7
Addenda

Doctor's Sister Dolly Reminisces*

We were a family of four children: two older brothers and two younger sisters. Minie was the second oldest, and I was the youngest. Our Mother and Father brought us up to be thrifty, outgoing, and good; we were in church or Sunday School every Sunday. Minie was President of the Epsworth League, an older group in our church.

We had our own orchestra: Wilbur, the oldest, played the trumpet; Minie played the cello; Grace played the piano; and I played the violin. On Sunday evenings, Minie and I played in a quartet in church. He loved also to play the piano. His teacher made him play many solos; he certainly had rhythm.

As a child, Minie loved animals. We had a cat and two rabbits; he had pigeons and white mice as well. He wrote poetry. I remember when he was very young, a poem was printed in the Sunday School paper. He liked all the sports; we made a rink in the back yard. I think he enjoyed skating and hockey especially, but perhaps baseball even better. He had a magic lantern and made his own wireless set. He and a friend would talk to each other in Morse code. I remember he woke us up one night: he had just heard the SOS when the Titanic sank.†

He spent many hours at the dentist's office. I remember he came home with a drill the dentist had lent him. When he was in college at Tufts, we were told he received the highest marks ever given in anatomy; however, he continued on as he had started and became a dentist.

All this time, Minie was interested in religion; he was always searching. As a young man, he and my mother heard a voice. I remember it was in the upper back hall. My mother said, "Minie, did you hear that?" And he answered, "Yes."

---

*Mrs. Laura Elliott, Doctor's sister "Dolly," offers the following stories about her brother.

†He also conveyed the news to the *Boston Globe*.

They often spoke about it. I remember when my mother "saw" her brother killed by a train. She even described the number of the train and time. Later the message came, and it was the exact train and time she had foreseen. They were very close.

When Minie met Swamiji, he was happy; and as the years passed, I know he was satisfied that he had found what he had been searching for. Swamiji's suggestions and advice always came out right.

I remember once Minie was out in the boat with my father and brother in a terrific storm, out in the middle of the bay. The man who lived across from us started out, but decided against it. We were on the porch, trying to see, but at times we couldn't even see the water, for all the hail and wind. Waiting inside, my mother was wringing her hands and walking from room to room. Mildred was most upset, too. When the storm was over, there the boat was, unbelievably, in the middle of the bay!

As soon as they returned to their home, Swamiji phoned and said right away, "You nearly got wet, didn't you?" He said he saw them, and he knew they were in trouble. These things you can never forget.

When Swamiji first came, in 1920, Minie was most anxious for me to meet this man from India. It was thoughtful and just like Minie, for, instead of going immediately to the home where Swamiji was, Minie drove around the boulevard, so that he could tell me more about him, and so I would feel less strange when I met him. Today it might have been different, but then to meet a Hindu in an orange robe and long hair was not an ordinary circumstance. I was most impressed, however, as he knew I would be, and have considered this a most important event in my life.

Several of us were in the car and going across the bridge on our way to a meeting in Boston, which Minie was to conduct, when suddenly the car skidded. He was driving, and I was in the back. Quietly, the car just stopped, as if a hand held it.

People seemed always to come to Minie for help and advice. You could count on him. Once he told me that Saints could see their own funerals. When we were at his funeral, that thought came to me, and I wondered if he were watching. Following the service at the grave site, a gust of wind suddenly came out of nowhere and blew down some of the flower sprays. I thought, "That's strange." It was as if something or someone was trying to get my attention. I looked up, and there I could see, for an instant, that what he told me was true.

Addenda

Ananda Mohan Lahiri
U.P. India

Mr. Minott W. Lewis
Box 266 The Hermitage
Encinitas, California U.S.A.

Sir, I owe you an apology for not writing to you so long. I could not get your letter so long due to the postal difficulty for delivering the same.

As you expected some interesting thing regarding Lahiri Mahasaya from me I have the pleasure to let you know one thing which is very interesting and philosophical and scientific too. I understand as you say you are practicing 'Kriya' very regularly. You must have learned something about "Kutasthe" — 'the universal inner sight.'

There is one universal power of sight which sees through everything without the instrument called the animal eye or "Chaksu Indriya." This power of sight is present everywhere, it is ever conscious, ever attentive, it is co-extensive with infinite space, it is space itself or cause of the idea of space, a real contact with it enables us to see everything through the human eyes but only in a limited way.

This 'kutastha' is 'Bisnu'. 'Bisnu' means that which is present in everything and all pervading. It is more active and quick than any radio power which is responsible for and is really at the bottom of all phenomena of television radio or transmission of sound.

Lahiri Mahasaya to a disciple foretold about the present discovery of science regarding all tele matters and radios that such things would come to pass as a thing of everyday experience. Such adept was he.

Now what was the secret which made him what he was? This must be more important to all who is at all interested in him. If a man can devote more than twelve hours of undivided attention a day on 'sthiti' (while having the habit of keeping a major share of attention on 'sthiti' for other hours — which is a kind of divided attention necessary for worldly life) he can perfectly go beyond his limitations to contact this 'Bisnu' or universal presence of God as ever-conscious infinite power of sight to see things on all sides, far, near and through. Lahiri Mahasaya was a practical man and hence he practised 'Kriya' a little over 12 hours in continuity at a time a day for more than 12 years to achieve his state of super-man and hence he could see through the universal eye of God. He predicted the independence of India and it occurred at the right time.

There is really only one eye—the very power of sight and this very eye has been referred to in the Holy Bible as 'the single eye!' "If thine eye be single then your whole body shall be full of light."

I have not explained what is 'sthiti'. What is "Sthiti?" It is rest — rest as conceived against its opposite, motion. Whatever moves — moves from point to point with rest at every point.* Every point has its existence in infinite space, the point being inseparably related to every other point and infinite space is only a creation of the divine power of the infinite eternal sight. In fact creation is only the seeing of the divinity. "Yada sa sikhata." The Veda says, "Then he saw."

So 'rest' or 'Sthiti' is at the back of every point of existence and so it is 'Bisnu' or at the back of universal existence also.

It is through 'Sthiti' or rest — however small it may be — that we contact God or all divine beings or the ascended ones. Thus we can see a Lahiri Mahasaya or a Christ in 'Kutastha' or we can become a Christ or a a Lahiri Mahasaya being constantly in touch with 'Kutastha' — the universal

---

*"He who perceives non-action in action, And action in non-action, Is the wisest."— Bhagavad Gita.

single eye, we can see the inner body. We are to take rest or find 'Sthiti' or manage self-surrender at 'Kutastha'.

This 'Kutastha' may be defined as a circle or better as a sphere whose centre is everywhere and circumference is nowhere, i.e., not to end by any limitation, it is a thing full of infinite power, power of sight, hearing etc. That is you can start with the center anywhere. It is more to be conceived than described. If it is attended closely — a 'Sthiti' however small it may be at the end of each respiration — as each 'sthiti' or rest at every point is universally inseparable from every other point — it gives us universal contact.

As rest or 'Sthiti' is inseparably everywhere (otherwise nothing could move) so 'Sthiti' is co-extensive with Bisnu, Kutastha or the universal divine eye. (We being finite its infinitude pours in us very gradually and sometimes all on a sudden.)

The secret key to Sthiti is innate in every man and is known specially through 'kriya'. A Brahmin is to contact the universal eye as the first thing to do or the first step before he can offer any worship and this is called 'Achman' or the 1st ablution of worship or any religious undertaking. You are under an able guide and hope you all success. May be as you expect someday we may meet together. Excuse me for the philosophy that I indulged in — it will require the brain of one Einstein to divine into it — I might have taxed your brain. I give you a glimpse of what could make Lahiri Mahasaya a Lahiri Mahasaya or what he was. It is no wonder that stories relating to Lahiri Mahasaya must be very wonderful as he identified himself deep with the very source of this mysterious creation. I am glad to explain you the cause of it and refrain from narrating the effects. When do you expect to come to India? Is it with Swamiji?

The ideal government is that which makes it possible for every man to have enough time for self-realization after arranging for everything worldly and necessary. India can establish this through Paramahansaji and through India,

[the] world will learn it — to establish peace and avoid all future war. So he is wanted in India for the great task. With divine love to you. All yours.

...I shall be glad to know if Paramahansaji would come to India as India wants him.

Sincerely,

Ananda Mohan Lahiri
[Grandson of Lahiri Mahasaya]

B. Lahiry
D 31/58, Madanpura,
Varanasi – 1
India
31st Jan., 1967

Mrs. Mildred Lewis
3062, First Avenue,
San Diego, California 92103, USA

My Dear Sister,

    [Mr.] ___, who visited me about a year back, has often written to me about you. I had not written so long because I felt that I had nothing of importance to write.
    I have received today a booklet, "The Life Story of Dr. M. W. Lewis," very kindly sent by ___; and I have finished reading it just now. He was a *real saint* both in his life and in his manner of leaving the body. Blessed are you, who lived with him as his devoted wife and "SAHA-DHARMINI" (one-in-spirit), and who saw him pass away in the manner described so wonderfully by you! He was an ideal householder and an ideal devotee. I can clearly see his genuine and pure heart, always ready to serve but never to dominate. Never to aspire for a position of honour even though it was his due, lest his resplendent brilliance of heavenly humility be eclipsed by the slightest trace of struggle for power! Always ready to help everybody, not from a high pedestal of a teacher, but as a fellow-traveller! Indeed, he was a rare man both as he lived as he died. ...
    Though I had never written to Dr. Lewis, he does not seem to be unknown and unacquainted. Indeed I would have considered it a privilege to know his lovable personality.
    I would be very glad to meet you if you come to India

and Varanasi. Please accept my best wishes and convey the blessings to your worthy son and daughter.

>With best greetings,
>Yours sincerely,
>
>B. Lahiry
>[Great-grandson of
>   Lahiri Mahashaya]

B. Lahiry
D31/58, Madanpura,
Varanasi – 1
India April 25, 1967

My Dear Sister,

Received your kind letter of April 8. ...
Doctor's life is now an open book to all who care to have a look at it. And you know best how advanced he was spiritually. So whether an omen was shown at his birth-time or not matters very little; and whether that omen could be correctly interpreted according to this culture or that is also very unimportant. Every child is a *potential* Christ, but it is how life unfolds that differentiates the Real one.

He lived the full life of householder, discharging all his family duties, yet went on progressing in the line of yoga, helping *unselfishly* all who came asking for help — physically — mentally and spiritually. This was the ideal of my Great-grandfather our beloved Lahiry Mahashaya. *He is a true disciple who works out in practical life the ideals preached and lived by the Guru,* not the one who merely repeats in words the ideals and lives contrary to those according to his own desires. Thus your husband was a true follower of my great grandfather — who practically lived His ideals.

As I did not hear from you for a long time, on the morning of April 17 I wrote to ___ enquiring about your health and welfare. And your letter came by the evening mail on the same day!

I am very glad to know that you and your family are in good health.

With best wishes and infinite love to you and your beloved family,

                              Yours sincerely,

                              B. Lahiry

Addenda
241

* © Copyright 1956 Dr. M. W. Lewis

Addenda